W9-BAL-259

AUTHENTIK®

Published by The Globe Pequot Press
246 Goose Lane, P.O. Box 480
Guilford, Connecticut 06437
www.globepequot.com

© 2007 Authentik Books
www.authentikbooks.com

Produced in France by Les Editions du Mont-Tonnerre
Text and illustrations copyright © Wilfried LeCarpentier

Authentik® Trademark, Wilfried LeCarpentier
4 bis Villa du Mont-Tonnerre, Paris XVe arrondissement
www.monttonnerre.com

ISBN 978-0-7627-4634-7
First Edition

Printed and bound in China

AUTHENTIK®

LES EDITIONS DU MONT-TONNERRE
Founder and Publisher: Wilfried LeCarpentier
Editor-at-Large: William Landmark
Managing Editor: Caroline Favreau

AUTHENTIK GOURMET PARIS
Restaurants, Wine and Food Consultant: Gérard Poirot
Project Editor: Nicola Mitchell
Copy Editors: Jessica Fortescue, Alison Culliford, Helen Stuart, Natasha Edwards and Sandra Iskander
Researcher: Jessica Phelan
Editorial Assistant: Jennifer Parker

Creative Director: Lorenzo Locarno
Artistic Director: Nicolas Mamet
Graphic Designer: Amélie Dommange
Layout Artist: Marie-Thérèse Gomez
Cover Design and Packaging: Nicolas Mamet
Cartographer: Map Resources
Map Illustrator: Kouakou
Pre-Press and Production: Studio Graph'M, Montrouge

GLOBE PEQUOT PRESS
President and Publisher: Scott Watrous
Editorial Director: Karen Cure

ACKNOWLEDGEMENTS
Special thanks to Marie-Christine Levet, Scott Watrous, Karen Cure, Gunnar Stenmar, Gérard Paulin, Pierre Jovanovic, Jacques Derey, Bruno de sa Moreira, Ian Irvine, Laura Tennant, Francesco Betti and Charles Walker

To M. DE CONTY, author of practical guides

"Dear Sir,

You have kindly requested a volume which would be entitled *The Pleasures of Paris* and which would contain the complete and reasoned survey of all the frolicsome things that constitute the "great attraction" of the capital of the universe.

That is to ask for the impossible : I will attempt it. More's the pity for you and for me !"

Alfred Delveau, *January 1867*

Uncover the Exceptional

The Authentik book collection was born out of a desire to explore beauty and craftsmanship in every domain and in whatever price bracket. The books describe the aesthetic essence of a city, homing in on modern-day artisans who strive for perfection and whose approach to their work is as much spiritual as commercial. Written by specialist authors, the guides delve deep into the heart of a capital and, as a result, are excellent companions for both locals and nomadic lovers of fine living. Their neat size, made to fit into a suit or back pocket, make them easy and discreet to consult, and their elegant design and insider selection of addresses will ensure that you get to the heart of the local scene and blend in perfectly with it. There is even a notebook at the back for some cerebral scribbling of your own. In all, Authentik Books are the perfect accessory for uncovering the exceptional, whether in the arts, fashion, design or gastronomy.

Wilfried LeCarpentier
Founder and Publisher

Rue Lepic, 18th

Contents

How to Use This Guide

Ever felt like jumping in a taxi at Roissy airport and saying, "Take me to the centre of things!?" Well, this book does the work of a very knowledgeable taxi driver.

Gourmet Paris consists of ten chapters of insider information on the city's culinary scene. It steers you to the finest restaurants and gourmet neighbourhoods; quotes star chefs on their favourite food and wine shops; gives advice on the best cookery schools such as Le Cordon Bleu and Le Ritz for honing in your own repertoire of recipes; and recommends the best kitchen and tableware stores.

The directory at the end of each chapter gives the addresses of the places mentioned, plus the details of other essential stops too numerous to include in the chapter. The maps at the back of the guide cover the principal streets of central Paris. Use the map references added to the addresses to find the general location of our listings.

The guide online

Using the **2D BAR CODE** below you can load all the addresses onto a mobile phone with Internet access. This unique aspect of the book enables you to travel extra light.

scan here

How to access content on your mobile phone

If your mobile phone has Internet access and a built-in camera go to

www.scanlife.com

Download the free software that allows your mobile phone to identify the bar code. Downloading takes less than one minute. Then go to your personal file icon, which will appear on your phone's menu screen and select the icon **Scanlife**. Next, point your camera at the 2D bar code. A sound confirms that the bar code has been recognized. You can then access the directories on your phone.

A NEW CULINARY AESTHETIC

Le Comptoir du Relais
9 carrefour de l'Odéon, 6th

Previous page: Mon Vieil Ami
69 rue Saint-Louis-en-l'Ile, 4th

I t's not easy being Paris. Unlike culinary upstarts such as London and Sydney, this city has a long-standing reputation to live up to. Fortunately, chefs know what is at stake and have been working hard in the past few years to prove themselves. Today it's safe to say that Paris has a more eclectic dining scene than ever, with cooks feeling less constrained by tradition and freer to express their personalities through their cooking. This renewed interest in good food has filtered down to some Parisians, who are signing up for lunchtime cooking classes, having heirloom vegetables delivered to their doors, and subscribing to ground breaking food magazines.

The euro syndrome

Higher prices since the advent of the euro mean that dining out is considered more of a treat, but this has encouraged excellence even at the lower end of the price scale. You can eat well in Paris for €30 per person, and the difference between a casual bistro and an establishment serving haute cuisine often lies more in the comfort of the surroundings than the food itself.

A new dining phenomenon

A sign of more price-conscious times is a new style of restaurant that has been dubbed '*bistronomique*'. Launched in the 1990s by several protégés of chef Christian Constant who trained with him at the Hôtel de Crillon, the 'gastronomic bistro' probably best represents Paris dining today. This group of young chefs applies haute cuisine techniques and regional know-how to humble products such as oxtail, pig cheeks and mackerel, resulting in country-style cooking with a sophisticated touch.

Bistronomique stars

Among the leaders of the pack are quick-tempered Yves Camdeborde at **Le Comptoir du Relais** in Saint-Germain and irascible Stéphane Jégo of **l'Ami Jean**, but they are now spawning offshoots as ever-younger chefs open small yet ambitious bistros with frequently changing, seasonally-led menus. A mini-trend is the 20-seat bistro run by a lone chef, with the spouse handling the front of house, as at **Le Temps au Temps** and **La Cerisaie**. To compensate for their long workdays, many bistros close for two or three days over the weekend, which can take visitors by surprise. Other gastronomic bistro stars include Sylvain Danière at **l'Ourcine**, André Le Letty at **l'Agassin** and Christophe Beaufront at **L' Avant-Goût**.

Master chef moves

The rarefied world of haute cuisine is also reaching out to the average diner with a (somewhat) more accessible style of restaurant. Joël Robuchon walked away from luxury dining at the peak of his career to re-emerge with **l'Atelier de Joël Robuchon**, in which elegant food inspired by France, Spain and Asia is served in tapas-style portions at a counter. In a radical statement, Alain Senderens transformed his landmark art nouveau restaurant Lucas Carton into the edgier **Senderens**, which has a fusion menu with suggested drinks to match each course and its own mezzanine tapas bar, too.

Experimental chef Pierre Gagnaire runs a seafood annex, **Gaya Rive Gauche**, while renowned Alsatian Antoine Westermann now oversees the bistro **Mon Vieil Ami** and the chic brasserie **Drouant**.

Alain Ducasse is in a category of his own, heading swish restaurants in Paris and Monte Carlo as well as the **Spoon**, **Food & Wine** chain, the historic bistros **Benoit** and **Aux Lyonnais**, the seafood restaurant **Rech**, and the Eiffel Tower's gastronomic restaurant **Le Jules Verne**. Ducasse takes criticism for spending more time on planes than in the kitchen, but he has trained a generation of young chefs.

01

Le Pré Verre
8 rue Thénard, 5th

International influences

The classic bistro with a predictable menu is becoming a rarity these days, as chefs experiment with foreign ingredients and new flavour or texture combinations. Inaki Aizpitarte at **Le Chateaubriand** might deconstruct a classic French dish such as *bœuf carottes*, serving cooked and raw beef spiked with Basque chili pepper alongside glazed and raw carrots and jellied bouillon. William Ledeuil at **Ze Kitchen Galerie** buys many of his ingredients in Chinatown, while Philippe Delacourcelle works Asian spices and smoked flavours into traditional French dishes at the excellent bistro **Le Pré Verre**. Young Turks are not by themselves: veteran Roland Durand has shared his passion for rare Asian ingredients at his sophisticated **Passiflore** for years.

Snacking takes off

Most of all, what has marked the past few years is a change in Parisian eating habits. Instead of tucking into a *steak-frites* with a glass of Gamay, office workers are more likely to buy sandwiches and salads in the snack shops that have sprung up all over the city, while executives tuck into noodles in the no-frills Japanese restaurants along rue Sainte-Anne in the 2nd *arrondissement*.

Prepared foods boom

Many Parisians still shop at the food markets and cook with fresh ingredients on weekdays, but the chain of frozen food shops Picard has become a standby even for TV chefs such as Julie Andrieu, who wrote the Picard cookbook. Food markets are adapting to the reality that both women and men work these days by opening in the afternoons in central areas such as the Bourse, and serving more prepared foods. Parisians can watch their take-away meals being prepared by a chef in **La Grande Epicerie du Bon Marché**'s food hall or buy kits of ready-prepped food to finish off at home in new shops such as **Kit à Bien Manger** and at Italian delis like **Pepone**.

Catering innovation

Crafty hosts bring their own serving dishes to gourmet delis such as **Bread & Roses** to have them filled with deluxe salads or tiramisu. The ultimate *traiteur* is probably **Fauchon**, which has a selection of take-away dishes that is glitzier than ever, at restaurant prices.

Quality control

We are growing more concerned with quality as a result of food scares and the burgeoning organic movement. An increasing number of foods come with labels guaranteeing their origins and quality, most commonly the Label Rouge and sometimes the Appellation d'Origine Contrôlée (AOC). The **Raspail organic market** on Sundays has always been popular with hippie-style wholefood lovers, but more modern organic grocery shops and juice bars are booming as well.

01

Chefs commonly list the origins of their meat, fish and even vegetables on the menu: only recently have vegetables shed their bit-part status in French cuisine to star on the menus of chefs such as Alain Passard and Alexandre Mathieu. Perhaps no one has done more for vegetable awareness than the charismatic market gardener **Joël Thiébault**, who sells his glorious heirloom vegetables at two Paris markets. Adopted by many a discriminating chef, his multicoloured carrots, striped beetroot and Chinese radishes can be delivered anywhere in Paris.

Home cooking revival

It often surprises outsiders that many Parisians lack confidence in the kitchen. This is partly a consequence of the May 1968 uprising in France, which led to women casting away their aprons and embracing processed and packaged food. A generation of Parisians grew up without home cooking and many are now trying to compensate with courses for novice

Le Kit à Bien Manger
1 rue de Berite, 6th

cooks at schools such as **l'Atelier des Chefs** and **l'Atelier de Fred**. Almost all fashionable chefs have published cookbooks, notably Christian Constant, Yves Camdeborde and Dominique Versini of **Casa Olympe**. Of the many food magazines, *Régal* best reflects changing times.

01

Television tuition

Television also has a role to play: the cable channel **Cuisine TV** broadcasts dubbed versions of Jamie Oliver, Nigella Lawson and Gordon Ramsay's shows, alongside its own stars such as the exuberant **Maïté**. France 3's **Bon Appétit Bien Sûr!** is presented by über-chef Joël Robuchon, who invites fellow chefs to demonstrate their innovative recipes. On M6, **Cyril Lignac** has been groomed as the French Jamie Oliver, even training his own group of French youths to run a restaurant in Paris, **Le Quinzième**, the equivalent of Oliver's London restaurant Fifteen.

Complicating the Parisian quest for competence in the kitchen, however, is the lack of space usually attributed to this room in a typical town apartment. Parisians have to be adept jugglers to reproduce the great chefs' dishes in their own homes.

RESTAURANTS, CAFES AND BARS

Le Meurice
228 rue de Rivoli, 1st

Previous page: Le Violon d'Ingres
135 rue Saint-Dominique, 7th

On a Sunday morning, jovial Parisians crowd into the scruffy wine bar **Le Baron Bouge** on rue Théophile Roussel, having done their shopping at the nearby **Aligre market** in the 12th *arrondissement*. The setting couldn't be simpler, with upturned wine casks serving as tables. The cheese plate is the real thing: Saint-Félicien so creamy that it collapses under the knife, slices of sharp *tomme*, and an aged, ash-coated goat's cheese.

This is the kind of uniquely French experience that most people hope for when they come to Paris. Down-to-earth cafés with basic but incredible food still exist in every *arrondissement*, but a more adventurous style of bistro has emerged that is keeping the dining scene exciting, often run by the young protegés of top chefs branching out on their own. Haute cuisine continues to thrive even in more money-conscious times, and many top chefs, such as Guy Savoy and Alain Dutournier, Pierre Gagnaire and Alain Senderens, have opened informal annexes or changed the style of their restaurants to make their cooking more accessible.

Cafés have updated their decors for the 21st century, sometimes with food to match. Even bars often turn out perfectly decent cooking. The key to eating well in Paris is to do your research before you go and keep your expectations in check. Like any capital city, Paris offers its share of rip-offs, but for the best chefs, cooking remains a labour of love.

Bistronomique: small is beautiful

The most promising trend in Paris is a cross between 'bistro' and 'gastronomic' and took root in the early 1990s, when Christian Constant was head chef at Le Crillon. Constant encouraged the young chefs who worked with him to open their own bistros rather than working their way through the grand hotels.

Yves Camdeborde was the most influential of these chefs, first at **La Régalade** and now at **Le Comptoir du Relais**, where the single nightly seating for the *prix fixe* dinner is booked up months in advance. What made his cooking different was the combination of haute cuisine technique and humble ingredients, such as sardines or even sheep's testicles. During the 1990s many Constant disciples followed suit, such as Christian Etchebest at **Le Troquet,** and Rodolphe Paquin at the **Repaire de Cartouche**. All these chefs draw on their regional roots to produce a sophisticated take on country cuisine; a perfect example is Etchebest's snails "in my grandmother's style", with lamb's lettuce, bacon, capers, pistachio vinaigrette and fried croutons. Now in their mid- to late thirties, these chefs are old enough to have spawned their own protégés, among them Stéphane Jégo at the Basque bistro **l'Ami Jean** and Sylvain Danière at **l'Ourcine**.

02

A few other young chefs have emerged on their own to run tiny bistros such as **Le Bistral**, popular for the great wines discovered by owner Alexandre Mathieu and chef Thierry Berlan. Another is **L'Agassin**, where André Le Letty, the former chef of the French foreign ministry, serves *canards au sang* (pressed duck) as good as those at the more expensive Tour d'Argent.

If the original gourmet bistros were found on the outskirts of Paris, there are now at least two or three in every *arrondissement*. Their menus change often, the choice of dishes is limited and the price rarely climbs above €40 for a three-course meal.

Fine dining

Add a zero to the bistro price figure and you're in an entirely different category, one in which the environment counts as much as the food on your plate. For an over-the-top experience there is still probably no better

Astrance
4 rue Beethoven, 16th

city than Paris, with its glittering settings, polished service and extraordinarily precise cooking. Haute cuisine is not standing still, as proved by Pascal Barbot, who worked alongside Passard before opening his minimalist, grey-coloured restaurant **Astrance**. His ethereal cooking draws on Asian ingredients and surprising sauces such as carrot cake butter, made by melting down the cake batter to extract the flavoured fat.

02

Pushing the limits of French cuisine with wild and complex flavour fusions is **Pierre Gagnaire**, who operates out of a sober dining room in the Hôtel Balzac. At the sumptuous **Le Meurice**, Yannick Alléno shows that restraint can have its place in contemporary French cuisine with dishes such as duck foie gras poached in Chambertin wine. Widely esteemed chef Alain Passard works wonders with vegetables from his kitchen garden at **l'Arpège**, daring to serve a simple dish of baked beetroot with aged balsamic vinegar as a starter.

If you enjoy a festive setting, aim for the second dining room at **Taillevent**, where you can choose to sit side-by-side on a banquette for some of the classiest people-watching in town. Like many haute cuisine restaurants, Taillevent has a much more affordable lunch menu at €70, wine not included.

Many leading chefs now offer alternatives to the classic fine dining experience, not only to keep up with the times but as a way of countering the financial risks involved in haute cuisine. Joël Robuchon turned his back on tradition to open l'**Atelier de Joël Robuchon**, where seating around a tapas-style bar in front of an open kitchen encourages conversation between the customers and staff. Alain Dutournier, who runs deluxe **Carré des Feuillants** off the Tuileries garden, followed Robuchon's path with another tapas place, **Pinxo**.

The first 'baby bistros' were opened by Michel Rostang and Guy Savoy, serving slightly pared-down versions of their classic dishes in more casual settings. Star Alsatian chef Antoine Westermann oversees the chic brasserie **Drouant** and the bistro **Mon Vieil Ami**, while the Roanne-based Michel Troisgros now has a Paris presence at **La Table du Lancaster**. The chef to have branched out the most is Alain Ducasse, whose latest acquisitions are **Le Jules Verne** at the Eiffel Tower and the seafood house **Rech**. Interestingly, Christian Constant has followed suit by converting his traditional restaurant **Le Violon d'Ingres** into a contemporary brasserie. He also runs the nostalgic bistro **Le Café Constant**, the fish bistro **Les Fables de la Fontaine**, and **Les Cocottes**, all four in rue Saint-Dominique in the 7th *arrondissement*.

Fast and healthy

For Parisians in search of fast and healthy options, the best is **Rose Bakery** on rue des Martyrs in the 9th *arrondissement,* a Franco-British café that serves mostly organic soups, salads, pizzettes and cakes – from carrot cake to lemon tart.

02

Cojean is a popular chain targeting Parisians looking for healthier lunch options. New juice bars seem to open weekly, among them the stark white, organic **Bioboa** and the flashily hued **Wanna Juice**. **Scoop** is an American-style sundae parlour with light lunch fare and an intimate salon upstairs. Look also for great Italian delis, including **Frascati**, **Mille Pâtes**, **Pasta Linea** and **Café Pepone**.

Cafés and bars

Cafés provide a flexible alternative to traditional French restaurants and bistros. The Costes brothers run some of the most stylish café-brasseries in town, such as **Café Marly** overlooking the Louvre's pyramid, and **Restaurant Georges** on top of the Centre Pompidou. Some neighbourhood cafés have dressed themselves up with plush chairs and trendy light fixtures. The food has not always followed suit, though prices have, especially outrageous mark-ups on wine, even for ordinary Beaujolais or Bordeaux.

Other cuisines

In the past 20 years, the number of international restaurants in Paris has multiplied, even if many adapt their cuisines (sometimes fairly drastically) to suit French tastes.

North African cuisine is well represented at restaurants such as **Chez Omar**, **404**, **L'Homme Bleu** and **Le Souk**, all of which dish up couscous or tagines with plenty of atmosphere. Best Japanese restaurants include **Wada,** on the rue de l'Arc de Triomphe near Etoile, **Kinugawa** on rue Saint-Philippe du Roule and rue du Mont Thabor, and **Aïda** a block away from Bon Marché, as well as **Isami** on the Ile Saint Louis. Of the hundreds of Italian restaurants in Paris, quite a few get it right, among them **La Taverna degli Amici**, **Sardegna a Tavola** and **Pasta e Basta**. Simple Laotian or Vietnamese restaurants are a good bet if you have a southeast Asian craving and can be found around avenue d'Ivry in Paris Chinatown.

Restaurant Georges,
Centre Pompidou
19 rue Beaubourg, 4th

For good cocktails and honest food, reliable bets are **Le Fumoir** near the Louvre, the mezzanine of the **Alcazar** on rue Mazarine, **Chez Prune** on Canal Saint Martin and the art nouveau **Café Charbon** on rue Oberkampf.

To end a night out in style, waltz into a bar in one of the city's palace hotels, such as the Ritz's **Hemingway Bar** or **Le Bar du Plaza Athénée**. The cocktails will cost a mint but, in places like these, that's beside the point. Other fashionable and lively bars open very late include **Le Forum** off Place de la Madeleine and **Le Café du Passage** in the shadows of Bastille. Smaller and less expensive are **Marlusse et Lapin** and the bohemian **Grand Hôtel de Clermont**, in Montmartre.

Le Chateaubriand
129 avenue Parmentier, 11th

Bistronomique: small is beautiful

L'Agassin
8 r Malar, 7th
Ⓜ La Tour Maubourg
Ⓒ 01 47 05 94 27
✠ 9-10/G10

Aux Lyonnais
32 r St-Marc, 2nd
Ⓜ Richelieu-Drouot
Ⓒ 01 42 96 65 04
✠ 7/N7

L'Avant-Goût
26 r Bobillot
Ⓜ Place d'Italie
Ⓒ 01 53 80 24 00
✠ Off map

Benoit
20 r St-Martin, 4th
Ⓜ Hôtel de Ville
Ⓒ 01 42 72 25 76
✠ 7/R9

Le Bistral
80 r Lemercier, 17th
Ⓜ Brochant
Ⓒ 08 99 78 21 82
✠ 2/K1

Le Café Constant
139 r St-Dominique, 7th
Ⓜ Ecole Militaire
Ⓒ 01 47 53 73 34
✠ 9/F11

La Cerisaie
70 bd Edgar Quinet, 14th
Ⓜ Edgar Quinet
Ⓒ 01 43 20 98 98
✠ 14/K7

Le Chateaubriand
129 av Parmentier, 11th
Ⓜ Goncourt
Ⓒ 01 43 57 45 95
✠ 8/W8

L'Ami Jean
27 r Malar, 7th
Ⓜ Invalides
Ⓒ 01 47 05 86 89
✠ 9-10/G10

Chez Michel
10 r de Belzunce, 10th
Ⓜ Gare du Nord
Ⓒ 01 44 53 06 20
✠ 3/Q3

Le Comptoir du Relais
9 cf de l'Odéon, 6th
Ⓜ Odéon
Ⓒ 01 43 29 12 05
✠ 11/N13

L'Ourcine
92 r Broca, 13th
Ⓜ Les Gobelins
Ⓒ 01 47 07 13 65
✠ 15/Q17

Le Pré Verre
8 r Thénard, 5th
Ⓜ Maubert Mutualité
Ⓒ 01 43 54 59 47
✠ 15/P14

La Régalade
49 av Jean Moulin, 14th
Ⓜ Alésia
Ⓒ 01 45 45 68 58
✠ Off map

Repaire de Cartouche
8 bd des Filles du Calvaire, 11th
Ⓜ St-Sébastien Froissart
Ⓒ 01 47 00 25 86
✠ 12/U10

Spoon, Food & Wine
14 r de Marignan, 8th
Ⓜ Franklin D. Roosevelt
Ⓒ 01 40 76 34 44
✠ 5-6/G7

Le Temps au Temps
13 r Paul-Bert, 11th
Ⓜ Faidherbe-Chaligny
Ⓒ 01 43 79 63 40
✠ 12/Y13

Le Troquet
21 r François-Bonvin, 15th
Ⓜ Sèvres Lecourbe
Ⓒ 01 45 66 89 00
✠ 13-14/G16

02

Fine dining

L'Ambroisie
9 pl des Vosges, 4th
Ⓜ St-Paul
Ⓒ 01 42 78 51 45
✛ 12/U12

Gaya Rive Gauche
44 r du Bac, 7th
Ⓜ Rue du Bac
Ⓒ 01 45 44 73 73
✛ 10/K12

Rech
62 av des Ternes, 17th
Ⓜ Ternes
Ⓒ 01 45 72 29 47
✛ 1/E4

L'Arpège
84 r de Varenne, 7th
Ⓜ Varenne
Ⓒ 01 47 05 09 06
alain-passard.com
✛ 10/I12

Le Jules Verne
Tour Eiffel
Champ de Mars, 7th
Ⓜ Ecole Militaire
Ⓒ 01 45 55 61 44
✛ 9/E12

Senderens
9 pl de la Madeleine, 8th
Ⓜ Madeleine
Ⓒ 01 42 65 22 90
✛ 6/K7

Astrance
4 r Beethoven, 16th
Ⓜ Passy
Ⓒ 01 40 50 84 40
✛ 9/B11

Le Meurice
228 r de Rivoli, 1st
Ⓜ Tuileries
Ⓒ 01 44 58 10 10
✛ 6/K8

La Table du Lancaster
7 r de Berri, 8th
Ⓜ George V
Ⓒ 01 40 76 40 18
✛ 5/F6

**L'Atelier de Joël
Robuchon**
5 r de Montalembert, 7th
Ⓜ Rue du Bac
Ⓒ 01 42 22 56 56
✛ 10/L11

Pierre Gagnaire
6 r Balzac, 8th
Ⓜ George V
Ⓒ 01 58 36 12 50
pierre-gagnaire.com
✛ 5/E6

Taillevent
15 r Lamennais, 8th
Ⓜ George V
Ⓒ 01 44 95 15 01
✛ 1-5/F5

Drouant
16-18 pl Gaillon, 2nd
Ⓜ Opéra
Ⓒ 01 42 65 15 16
drouant.com
✛ 6/M7

Pinxo
9 r d'Alger, 1st
Ⓜ Tuileries
Ⓒ 01 40 20 72 00
lutetia-paris.com
✛ 6/L8

Le Violon d'Ingres
135 r St-Dominique, 7th
Ⓜ Ecole Militaire
Ⓒ 01 45 55 15 05
leviolondingres.com
✛ 9/F11

Fast and healthy

Bioboa
3 r Danielle Casanova, 1st
Ⓜ Pyramides
Ⓒ 01 42 61 17 67
⊕ 6/M8

Frascati
14 r de Turenne, 4th
Ⓜ Saint-Paul
Ⓒ 01 42 77 27 42
⊕ 11-12/T11

La Pizzetta
22 av Trudaine, 9th
Ⓜ Anvers
Ⓒ 01 48 78 14 08
⊕ 3/O3

Café Pepone
10 r Lepic, 18th
Ⓜ Blanche
Ⓒ 01 42 55 60 15
⊕ 2/M2

Le Jardin des Pâtes
33 bd Arago, 13th
Ⓜ Gobelins
Ⓒ 01 45 35 93 67
⊕ 15/Q17

Rose Bakery
46 r des Martyrs, 9th
Ⓜ Saint-Georges
Ⓒ 01 42 82 12 80
⊕ 3/O4

Cojean
17 bd Haussmann, 8th
Ⓜ Madeleine
Ⓒ 01 47 70 22 65
cojean.fr
⊕ 2-6/K5

Lili's Brownies Café
35 r Dragon, 6th
Ⓜ St-Germain-des-Prés
Ⓒ 01 45 49 25 03
⊕ 10/M13

Scoop
154 r St-Honoré, 1st
Ⓜ Louvre-Rivoli
Ⓒ 01 42 60 31 84
scoopcafe.com
⊕ 11/O10

Colette
213 r St-Honoré, 1st
Ⓜ Tuileries
Ⓒ 01 55 35 33 90
colette.fr
⊕ 6/L8

Mille Pâtes
5 r des Petits-Champs, 1st
Ⓜ Pyramides
Ⓒ 01 42 96 03 04
⊕ 7/N8

Le Village
12 r Broca, 13th
Ⓜ Gobelins
Ⓒ 01 43 31 73 85
⊕ 15/P17

La Ferme Opéra
55 r St-Roch, 1st
Ⓜ Pyramides
Ⓒ 01 40 20 12 12
⊕ 6/M8

Pasta Linea
9 r de Turenne, 4th
Ⓜ Saint-Paul
Ⓒ 01 42 77 62 54
⊕ 11-12/T11

Wanna Juice
65 r St-André-des-Arts, 6th
Ⓜ Odéon
Ⓒ 01 46 34 11 90
wannajuice.com
⊕ 11/O13

Cafés and bars

Alcazar
62 r Mazarine, 6th
Ⓜ Mabillon
Ⓒ 01 53 10 19 99
alcazar.fr
⊕ 11/N12

Bar 30
Sofitel Le Faubourg
15 r Boissy D'Anglas, 8th
Ⓜ Concorde
Ⓒ 01 44 94 14 14
⊕ 6/J7

Le Bar du Plaza Athénée
25 av Montaigne, 8th
Ⓜ Alma-Marceau
Ⓒ 01 53 67 66 65
plaza-athenee-paris.com
⊕5/F8

Le Baron Bouge
1 r Théophile Roussel,
12th
Ⓜ Ledru Rollin
Ⓒ 01 43 43 14 32
⊕ 16/W14

Café Charbon
109 r Oberkampf, 11th
Ⓜ Parmentier
Ⓒ 01 43 57 55 13
⊕ 8/W8

Café Marly
93 r de Rivoli, 1st
Ⓜ Louvre
Ⓒ 01 49 26 06 60
⊕ 6/M9

Le Café du Passage
12 r de Charonne, 11th
Ⓜ Ledru Rollin
Ⓒ 01 49 29 97 64
⊕ 12/W12

Chez Prune
36 r Beaurepaire, 10th
Ⓜ Jacques-Bonsergent
Ⓒ 01 42 41 30 47
⊕ 7-8/T7

Le Colibri
35 r Véron, 18th
Ⓜ Blanche
Ⓒ 01 42 60 59 22
⊕ 3/N1

Le Forum
4 bd Malesherbes, 8th
Ⓜ Madeleine
Ⓒ 01 42 65 37 86
⊕ 6/L8

Le Fumoir
6 r de l'Amiral Coligny, 1st
Ⓜ Louvre-Rivoli
Ⓒ 01 42 92 00 24
⊕ 11/O10

**Grand Hôtel
de Clermont**
18 r Véron, 18th
Ⓜ Abbesses
Ⓒ 01 46 06 40 99
⊕ 3/N1

**Hemingway Bar
at the Ritz**
15 pl Vendôme, 1st
Ⓜ Madeleine
Ⓒ 01 43 16 30 30
⊕ 6/L8

Marlusse et Lapin
14 r Germain Pilon, 18th
Ⓜ Abbesses
Ⓒ 01 42 59 17 97
⊕ 3/N2

Restaurant Georges
Centre Pompidou
19 r Beaubourg, 4th
Ⓜ Rambuteau
Ⓒ 01 44 78 47 99
⊕ 11/R10

International cuisine

404
69 r des Gravilliers, 3rd
Ⓜ Arts et Métiers
Ⓒ 01 42 74 57 81
✛ 7/R9

Aïda
1 r Pierre Leroux , 7th
Ⓜ Vaneau
Ⓒ 01 43 06 14 18
✛ 14/J14

Chez Omar
47 r de Bretagne, 3rd
Ⓜ Temple
Ⓒ 01 42 72 36 26
✛ 7-8/T9

Pasta e Basta
58 r du Javelot, 13th
Ⓜ Tolbiac
Ⓒ 01 44 24 54 84
✛ Off map

L'Homme Bleu
55bis r Jean-Pierre
Timbaud, 11th
Ⓜ Parmentier
Ⓒ 01 48 07 05 63
✛ 8/W8

Isami
4 quai d'Orléans, 4th
Ⓜ Pont Marie
Ⓒ 01 40 46 06 97
✛ 11/R13

Kinugawa
9 r du Mont Thabor, 1st
Ⓜ Tuileries
Ⓒ 01 42 60 65 07
✛ 6/K8

Kunitoraya
39 rue Ste-Anne, 1st
Ⓜ Pyramides
Ⓒ 01 47 03 33 65
kunitoraya.com
✛ 7/N8

Sardegna a Tavola
1 r de Cotte, 12th
Ⓜ Ledru Rollin
Ⓒ 01 44 75 03 28
✛ 16/X14

Le Souk
1 r Keller, 11th
Ⓜ Ledru-Rollin
Ⓒ 01 49 29 05 08
✛ 12/W12

La Taverna degli Amici
16 r du Bac, 7th
Ⓜ Rue du Bac
Ⓒ 01 42 60 37 74
✛ 10/K12

Wada
19 r de l'Arc de Triomphe,
17th
Ⓜ Ternes
Ⓒ 01 44 09 79 19
✛ 1/D4

02

See page 9
to scan the
directory

GOURMET
NEIGHBOURHOODS

Cafés Verlet
256 rue Saint-Honoré, 1st

Previous page: La Grande Epicerie du Bon Marché
38 rue de Sèvres, 7th

I t's hard to walk down any Paris street without being inexorably drawn into its food shops: the *boulanger* who turns out three fresh batches of *baguettes à l'ancienne* every day, the *fromagère* who ages her cheeses with tender care, the butcher who puts as much love into a humble *steak haché* as a stuffed and rolled veal roast, the *chocolatier* who spikes his ganaches with thyme, violet or ginger.

03

Every neighbourhood has its traditional food shops and markets, some undoubtedly have a greater share than others. The place de la Bourse now has an afternoon food market twice a week. The areas around the Champs-Elysées, the Louvre and Opéra are not outstanding for food shopping, though there is always a chance of coming across a mouth-watering boutique such as **Cafés Verlet** or **Jabugo Ibérico & Co**. Food shops are also a little scarce in some of the outlying *arrondissements*, such as the 19th and 20th and parts of the 16th and 17th. If you plan on doing some cooking, aim to stay somewhere near a market street, which will be open every day except Sunday afternoon and Monday (plan ahead or you might find yourself at a bleak Franprix supermarket).

Saint-Germain-des-Prés

Arguably the best food neighbourhood in the city is Saint-Germain, home not only to **La Grande Epicerie du Bon Marché** and the **Raspail organic market** but also to a multitude of small food shops run by passionate artisans. Chic shops with a special focus have replaced vegetable stalls along the market streets rue de Seine and rue de Buci, but the quality remains high.

Look in particular for the sleek cheese shop **Fromagerie 31**, with its own little *bar à fromages*, and the gourmet deli/restaurant **Da Rosa** focusing on Spanish *jabugo* and vintage Port wines. Another extraordinary cheese shop in the area is **Barthélemy**. What is most remarkable about this area, though, is the concentration of pastry and chocolate shops.

Within a few minutes' walk of each other are the boutiques of star pâtissiers **Pierre Hermé**, **Sadaharu Aoki** and **Gérard Mulot**, while chocolatiers such as **Patrick Roger** and **Pierre Marcolini** turn out intense ganaches and chocolate sculptures. You'll also find branches of **Ladurée** and **Debauve et Gallais**, a chocolate shop founded in 1800. Bread doesn't take a back seat either: try the chewy *baguette à l'ancienne* at **Au Pain Retrouvé** or the organic rye and seed loaf at **Bread & Roses** on rue de Fleurus.

The Latin Quarter

If the Latin Quarter is best known for the kebab shops that cater to students and tourists, a stroll into the more residential parts of the area yields yet other rewards. A small neighbourhood market takes place in **Place Maubert** three times a week – look for Provençal olives, farm-fresh chicken and dairy products, and an enticing organic produce stand.

03

Past the crêpe stands at the top of rue Mouffetard is a cobbled market street that has branches of the **Androuët** and **Quatrehomme** cheese shops, two gleaming fishmongers, the friendly local wine shop **La Fontaine aux Vins** and the chocolate shop **Nicolson**, which sells Berthillon ice cream. There are produce stands at the bottom of the street, but you'll need to pick and choose carefully. Continue to the end of rue Monge and you'll spot a queue snaking out of the **Boulanger de Monge**, which serves 2,000 clients daily.

Around the Eiffel Tower

Further towards the Eiffel Tower, the market street **rue Cler** is at the centre of another food-minded neighbourhood, known as le Gros Caillou, with the gourmet charcuterie **Davoli** and excellent cheese shop **Marie-Anne Cantin**. On rue Saint Dominique, a reliable wine shop is **Le Repaire de Bacchus**, run by the

Rue Montorgueil, 2th

English-speaking Antoine Menillet, while Jean-Marie Boedec at **Les Viandes du Champ de Mars** has a display of top-quality French meat.

A down-to-earth street market takes place on Wednesday and Sunday mornings under the above-ground Métro line along **boulevard de Grenelle**. To complete the makings of a picnic on the Champs de Mars, stop into a little-known branch of the **Poilâne** bakery just past the end of the market.

03

Les Halles

Though no longer the centre of the wholesale food trade, Les Halles retains a few remnants of its glory days. Explore the streets around the Forum des Halles shopping mall (particularly rue Coquillière, rue Montmartre and rue Tiquetonne) to find restaurant quality kitchenware, whole lobes of foie gras and three-kilogram bags of Valrhona chocolate. The cobbled **rue Montorgueil** is the only food market in the area and as a result it's always packed. Take in the scene from one of the many café terraces before treating yourself to an Ali Baba at the oldest patisserie in Paris, **Stohrer**. A pre-cursor to the baba au rhum, the Ali Baba is filled with pastry cream and raisins. This market has fine cheese shops, fishmongers and *primeurs* (greengrocers), along with one of the city's best butchers, **Alain Tribolet**.

Tang Frères
48 avenue d'Ivry, 13th

Asian supermarkets

If you ever start craving the bright, clean flavours of Asian food, head to the two main Chinese neighbourhoods: avenue de Choisy and avenue d'Ivry in the 13th *arrondissement*, and multicultural Belleville in the 11th. By far the biggest Asian supermarket is **Tang Frères** on avenue d'Ivry, which supplies many of the city's restaurants. Go here to find everything from fresh Thai basil and kaffir lime leaves to Tianjin preserved vegetable, used in Sichuan cooking. For a slightly less overwhelming Asian supermarket try **Paris Store Belleville**, then head up rue de Belleville to find smaller Asian shops. There is also a small cluster of Chinese restaurants and food shops in the 3rd, along rue au Maire. If you have a sushi craving that no Paris restaurant can satisfy, visit the Japanese supermarket **Kioko** near the Opéra Garnier for all the ingredients you need, with the exception of the raw fish. This shop has an impressive array of products to satisfy the area's homesick Japanese, even gourmet *koshi-hikari* rice.

03

Where to sleep

Though every neighbourhood has its highlights, it pays to be in the thick of the action. At the **Hôtel du Relais Saint-Germain** guests are entitled to a coveted dinner reservation at Yves Camdeborde's Le Comptoir de Relais, which otherwise requires a six-month wait. **Le Relais Christine**, also in Saint-Germain, is ideally placed for dining and shopping. A few steps from the Bon Marché is **Le Placide**, a boutique hotel with sleek rooms. The **Five Hotel**, with seductive lighting and a courtyard room with its own Jacuzzi, is about equidistant between rue Mouffetard market and Chinatown. More classic is the **Hôtel du Panthéon**, which is within easy reach of the Latin Quarter's best cafés and bistros.

For ease of dining at L'Atelier de Joël Robuchon, which does not take reservations, stay at the **Hôtel du Pont Royal** next door. In the Marais, the **Hôtel du Petit Moulin**, designed by Christian Lacroix, is close to the food shops on rue de Bretagne and rue Montorgueil. Set in a former brothel in the 9th, **Hôtel Amour** has rooms decorated by artists and its own stylish restaurant. The **Terrass Hôtel** has outstanding views from atop the butte Montmartre and the excellent Le Diapason restaurant, with the terrace that gives the hotel its name.

Hôtel du Petit Moulin
29/31 rue de Poitou, 3rd

03

Montmartre

Just below Montmartre, rue des Martyrs has become a gourmet haven even if it's not officially a market street. A highlight is **Arnaud Delmontel**, whose bread is as well crafted as his pastries. Across the street is **Rose Bakery**, which has been creating a buzz with its British-inspired, mostly organic cakes and savoury food. Heading up to Montmartre, rue des Abbesses is home to **Fromagerie Marie Bocquet**, the bakery **Le Grenier à Pain** and an intimate wine bar, **Caves des Abbesses**. Walk down the market street rue Lepic and have a coffee at **Les Deux Moulins**, which appeared in the Jean Jacques Jeunet film *Amélie* starring Audrey Tautou, or at **Lux Bar** across the street.

Saint-Germain-des-Prés

Barthélemy
51 r de Grenelle, 7th
Ⓜ Rue de Bac
Ⓒ 01 45 48 56 75
✛ 10/L13

Bread & Roses
7 r de Fleurus, 6th
Ⓜ Rennes
Ⓒ 01 42 22 06 06
✛ 14/M15

Da Rosa
62 r de Seine, 6th
Ⓜ Mabillon
Ⓒ 01 40 51 00 09
✛ 11/N12

Debauve et Gallais
30 r des Sts-Pères, 7th
Ⓜ St-Germain-des-Prés
Ⓒ 01 42 84 10 75
✛ 10/M11

Fromagerie 31
64 r de Seine, 6th
Ⓜ Mabillon
Ⓒ 01 43 26 50 31
✛ 11/N13

Gérard Mulot
2 r Lobineau, 6th
Ⓜ Odéon
Ⓒ 01 43 86 85 77
✛ 11/N13

**La Grande Epicerie
du Bon Marché**
38 r de Sèvres, 7th
Ⓜ St-Sulpice
Ⓒ 01 44 39 81 00
lagrandeepicerie.fr
✛ 10/L13

Kusmi Thé
56 r de Seine, 6th
Ⓜ Mabillon
Ⓒ 01 46 34 29 06
kusmitea.com
✛ 11/N12

Ladurée
21 r Bonaparte, 6th
Ⓜ St-Germain-des-Prés
Ⓒ 01 44 07 64 87
laduree fr
✛ 10/M11

Au Pain Retrouvé
81 r de Rennes, 6th
Ⓜ Sèvres Bablyone
Ⓒ 01 45 48 26 33
✛ 14/L14

Patrick Roger
108 bd St Germain, 6th
Ⓜ St-Germain-des-Prés
Ⓒ 01 43 29 38 42
✛ 10/L12

Pierre Hermé
72 r Bonaparte, 6th
Ⓜ St-Germain-des-Prés
Ⓒ 01 43 54 47 77
pierreherme.com
✛ 10/M13

Pierre Marcolini
89 r de Seine, 6th
Ⓜ Mabillon
Ⓒ 01 44 07 39 07
✛ 11/N12

Raspail market
*Tue, Fri and Sun 8am-
1.30pm (organic on Sun)*
bd Raspail/
r du Cherche-Midi, 6th
Ⓜ Rennes
✛ 14/L14

Sadaharu Aoki
35 r de Vaugirard, 6th
Ⓜ Rennes
adaharuaoki.com
✛ 14/K15

The Latin Quarter

Androuët
134 r Mouffetard, 5th
Ⓜ Censier Daubenton
Ⓒ 01 45 87 85 05
androuet.com
⊕ 15/Q17

La Fontaine aux Vins
107 r Mouffetard, 5th
Ⓜ Censier Daubenton
Ⓒ 01 43 31 41 03
⊕ 15/Q17

Place Maubert market
*Tue, Thur and Sat 8am-
1.30pm*
Pl Maubert, 5th
⊕ 15/Q14

Boulanger de Monge
123 r Monge, 5th
Ⓜ Censier Daubenton
Ⓒ 01 43 37 54 20
leboulangerdemonge.com
⊕ 15/Q17

Nicolsen
112 r Mouffetard, 5th
Ⓜ Censier Daubenton
Ⓒ 01 43 36 78 04
⊕ 15/Q17

Quatrehomme
118 r Mouffetard, 5th
Ⓜ Censier Daubenton
Ⓒ 01 45 35 13 19
⊕ 15/Q17

03

Around the Eiffel Tower

Le Café Constant
139 r St-Dominique, 7th
Ⓜ École Militaire
Ⓒ 01 47 53 73 34
⊕ 9/F11

Grenelle market
*Wed and Sun 8am-
1.30pm*
bd de Grenelle, 15th
Ⓜ La Motte-Picquet-
Grenelle
⊕ 9-13/D14

Le Repaire de Bacchus
122 r St-Dominique, 7th
Ⓜ Ecole Militaire
Ⓒ 01 45 51 77 21
⊕ 9/F11

Davoli
34 r Cler, 7th
Ⓜ Ecole Militaire
Ⓒ 01 45 51 23 41
davoli-paris.fr
⊕ 9-10/G11

Marie-Anne Cantin
12 r du Champ de Mars,
7th
Ⓜ Ecole Militaire
Ⓒ 01 45 50 43 94
cantin.fr
⊕ 9/F12

**Les Viandes du Champ
de Mars**
122 r St-Dominique, 7th
Ⓜ Ecole Militaire
Ⓒ 01 47 05 53 52
⊕ 9/F11

**Les Fables de la
Fontaine**
131 r St-Dominique, 7th
Ⓜ Ecole Militaire
Ⓒ 01 44 18 37 55
⊕ 9/F11

Poilâne
49 bd de Grenelle, 15th
Ⓜ Dupleix
Ⓒ 01 45 79 11 49
poilane.fr
⊕ 13/D14

Le Violon d'Ingres
135 r St-Dominique, 7th
Ⓜ Ecole Militaire
Ⓒ 01 45 55 15 05
leviolondingres.com
⊕ 9/F11

Les Halles

Alain Tribolet
54 r Montorgueil, 2nd
Ⓜ Etienne Marcel
☏ 01 42 33 04 06
✛ 7/P9

E. Dehillerin *(cookware)*
51 r J-J Rousseau, 1st
Ⓜ Palais-Royal
☏ 01 42 36 53 13
e-dehillerin.fr
✛ 7/O9

G. Detou *(baking supplies)*
58 r Tiquetonne, 2nd
Ⓜ Etienne Marcel
☏ 01 42 36 54 67
✛ 7/Q9

**Le Comptoir
de la Gastronomie**
34 r Montmartre, 1st
Ⓜ Les Halles
☏ 01 42 33 31 32
✛ 7/P8

Foie Gras de Luxe
26 r Montmartre, 1st
Ⓜ Les Halles
☏ 01 42 36 14 73
✛ 7P8

Stohrer
51 r Montorgueil, 2nd
Ⓜ Etienne Marcel
☏ 01 42 33 38 20
stohrer.fr
✛ 7/P9

Montmartre

Arnaud Delmontel
39 r des Martyrs, 9th
Ⓜ Saint-Georges
☏ 01 48 78 29 33
arnaud-delmontel.com
✛ 3/O4

Les Deux Moulins
15 r Lepic, 18th
Ⓜ Blanche
☏ 01 42 54 90 50
✛ 2/M2

Lux Bar
12 r Lepic, 18th
Ⓜ Blanche
☏ 01 46 06 05 15
✛ 2/M2

Les Cakes de Bertrand
7 r Bourdaloue, 9th
Ⓜ Notre-Dame-de-Lorette
☏ 01 40 16 16 28
lescakesdebertrand.com
✛ 3/N4

Fromagerie Bocquet
32 r des Abbesses, 18th
Ⓜ Abbesses
☏ 01 42 52 96 27
✛ 3/N1

A la Mère de Famille
35 r du Fbg Montmartre, 9th
Ⓜ Le Pelletier
☏ 01 47 70 83 69
lameredefamille.com
✛ 3-7/O5

Caves des Abbesses
43 r Abbesses, 18th
Ⓜ Abbesses
☏ 01 42 52 81 54
✛ 3/N1

Le Grenier à Pain
38 r des Abbesses, 18th
Ⓜ Abbesses
☏ 01 46 06 41 81
✛ 3/N1

Rose Bakery
46 r des Martyrs, 9th
Ⓜ Saint-Georges
☏ 01 42 82 12 80
✛ 3/O4

Asian supermarkets

Kioko
46 r des Petits Champs, 2nd
Ⓜ Pyramides
Ⓣ 01 42 61 33 66
kioko.fr
⊕ 7/N8

Paris Store Belleville
10 bd de Belleville, 19th
Ⓜ Belleville
Ⓣ 01 42 06 98 44
⊕ 8/X7

Tang Frères
48 av d'Ivry, 13th
Ⓜ Porte de Choisy
Ⓣ 01 45 70 80 00
⊕ Off map

Where to sleep

Five Hotel
3 r Flatters, 5th
Ⓜ Les Gobelins
Ⓣ 01 43 31 74 21
thefivehotel.com
⊕ Off map

Hôtel du Petit Moulin
29/31 r du Poitou, 3rd
Ⓜ St-Sébastien Froissart
Ⓣ 01 42 74 10 10
paris-hotel-petitmoulin.com
⊕ 12/I10

Le Placide
6 r St-Placide, 6th
Ⓜ Sèvres Babylone
Ⓣ 01 42 84 34 60
leplacidehotel.com
⊕ 14/K14

Hôtel Amour
8 r de Navarin, 9th
Ⓜ Notre-Dame-de-
Lorette
Ⓣ 01 48 78 31 80
hotelamour.com
⊕ 3/N3

Hôtel du Pont Royal
5 r Montalembert, 7th
Ⓜ Rue du Bac
Ⓣ 01 42 84 70 00
⊕ 10/L11

Le Relais Christine
3 r Christine, 6th
Ⓜ Mabillon
Ⓣ 01 40 51 60 80
relais-christine.com
⊕ 11/O12

Hôtel du Panthéon
19 pl du Panthéon, 5th
Ⓜ Cardinal Lemoine
Ⓣ 01 43 54 32 95
hoteldupantheon.com
⊕ 15/P15

**Hôtel du Relais
Saint-Germain**
9 cf de l'Odéon, 6th
Ⓜ Odéon
Ⓣ 01 43 29 12 05
⊕ 11/N13

Terrass Hôtel
12-14 r Joseph-de-
Maistre, 18th
Ⓜ Blanche
Ⓣ 01 46 06 72 85
terrass-hotel.com
⊕ 2/M1

03

See page 9
to scan the
directory

FINE FOODS
AND CONDIMENTS

Fauchon
24, 26, 30 place de la Madeleine, 8th

Previous page: Da Rosa
62, rue de Sèvres, 6th

When Parisians serve foie gras, they are likely to perch a slice without crushing it on toasted bread and sprinkle the liver with *fleur de sel* de Noirmoutier, which they believe is more delicate than *fleur de sel* from the Camargue. In bistros, they might add a modern flourish such as a dab of fig jam or mango chutney.

04

Sharing the knowledge

Food snobbism? Not really, as the aim is not to show off but to make each meal as pleasurable as possible. The more you know about your food, the more enjoyable it becomes, and Parisian food shops, particularly the small ones, staffed by knowledgeable and often passionate people, excel at bridging the gap between producer and consumer. When the chocolatier who makes those gem-like ganaches is the one who serves you, they can't help but inspire. No wonder Parisians are docile when queueing for luxury foods at boutiques such as **Da Rosa** or **Pierre Hermé**'s two pâtisseries and the bread shops of Christophe Vasseur, **Du Pain et des Idées.**

Legendary food halls

Paris has its food emporiums, such as Fauchon, Hédiard and La Grande Epicerie du Bon Marché, and these are best visited for specific products or to admire the artfulness of the displays. Both Hédiard and Fauchon were founded by former street merchants in the late 19th century: Ferdinand Hédiard opened his first Parisian store, the "Comptoirs d'épices et de colonies", in 1854, and Auguste Fauchon opened his stand in the Madeleine market in 1885. Temples of gastronomic exoticism, they cultivated a taste for foreign goods and luxury French fare at a time when pineapples were a revelation (Alexandre Dumas famously tasted his first one chez Hédiard). Today, **Hédiard** defies current trends by touting out-of-season produce and stocks some of the most richly flavoured jams, candied fruits and *pâtes de fruits* in town. Its tea counter also attests to its founder's vicarious love of faraway lands – he was known as the immobile traveller.

Hédiard's neighbour on Place de la Madeleine, **Fauchon,** has tried to establish a modern identity and now has a striking pink-and-white decor, savoury goods by chic former private chef Fumiko Kono and some of the most avant-garde pastries in Paris. It has opened a contemporary *boulangerie* for quick, light meals that suit the modern Parisian lifestyle.

At the Bon Marché department store, **La Grande Epicerie** seems to have everything you could hope for in a gourmet food hall. This is one of the very few places in Paris where you'll find rare breeds of chicken such as the *coucou de Rennes* (favoured by top chefs), and the wine section is well presented and its staff helpful. **Lafayette Gourmet,** its Right Bank equivalent, can be fun for a snack at one of the counters and the fresh meat is irreproachable. Lesser known, but worth a visit if you can't resist gourmet supermarkets, is the well-stocked **Inno** in Montparnasse.

04

Gourmet grocers

For the crème de la crème of French foods, however, it's always a good idea to seek out more specialist shops. Small gourmet grocers *(épiceries)*, often found in market streets, give you an idea of what Hédiard and Fauchon might have been like in their early days. In Montmartre's rue Lepic, **Le Comptoir Colonial** sells treasures from the former French colonies, such as pineapple jam, Mauritian coffee and Tahitian rum.

Nearby, the shop **Appellations d'Origine** is mainly dedicated to products with the AOC (Appellation d'Origine Contrôlée) label. Originally created for wines as a guarantee of origin and quality, this label is now applied to foods, including Espelette peppers

Hédiard
21 place de la Madeleine, 8th

from the Basque region, French olive oils and walnuts from Grenoble. José Da Rosa opened his *épicerie*-restaurant **Da Rosa** in Saint-Germain in 2003 to showcase the first-class products he had sourced for top French chefs. You'll find spice mixes from Olivier Roellinger in Cancale and Aquitaine caviar, alongside deluxe smoked salmon and Spanish ham, which can be sampled on his tapas-style menu.

On the Ile Saint Louis, **l'Epicerie** sells an inventive range of jams, mustards, flavoured oils and vinegars made especially for this shop and beautifully packaged. Look for honey-apricot vinegar and strawberry-chocolate jam. On rue Lecourbe, whose food shops are gradually disappearing, Valérie Gentil opened **Beau et Bon** to display her gourmet finds from all over France. Try the Banyuls vinegar, a staple for Basque chefs.

Luxury foods

The French go wild for luxury foods at Christmas and New Year, but foie gras, smoked salmon and caviar (or at least salmon or herring roe) are also year-round treats. For foie gras, some of the major labels to be found in Paris are **Ducs de Gascogne**, **Lafitte** and **Labeyrie**. Lesser known are **Comptoir Corrézien**, **Comptoir de la Gastronomie** and **Foie Gras de Luxe**, all of which are popular with chefs for their high quality and fair prices. Look for foie gras with a label certifying that it comes from the southwest of France, *Indication Géographique Protégée (IGP) canard à foie gras du Sud-Ouest*. Alsace also produces good foie gras, albeit in much smaller quantities.

Catering to luxury tastes since 1920, **Petrossian** in the 7th is best known for its caviar and smoked salmon, though it also sells foie gras. The fresh truffle season is short, from November to March, but **Terres de Truffes** and **La Maison de la Truffe**, both near Madeleine, stock winter or (less fragrant) summer truffles and truffle preserves all year-round.

Oils, honeys and condiments

More affordable, but perhaps just as luxurious, are French oils and condiments. The **Maille** boutique on Place de la Madeleine releases seasonal collections of flavoured mustards, as well as vinegars, oils and cornichons. France's olive oil production is small, but the best French olive oils, particularly from Les Baux de Provence and Nice, are among the finest in the world. You can find a selection at **A l'Olivier** in the Marais and at **Sur les Quais** in the Marché d'Aligre. For more unusual oils, visit the tiny shop **Huilerie Leblanc** in the 6th, which stocks walnut oil from the family's Burgundy estate along with such novelties as pistachio, pecan and pine nut oils. Several Paris shops are dedicated to honey, including **Les Ruchers du Roy** in the Marais.

Spices, teas and coffees

The interest in spices is growing, and nowhere has a fresher selection than the boutique **Goumanyat & Son Royaume** in the 3rd. If you have a taste for quality teas, you will find plenty to interest you at **Mariage Frères**, **Les Contes de Thé** and **Le Palais des Thés**. The elitist and very expensive **Maison des Trois Thés**, off Place Monge in the 5th, offers the best choice of Chinese teas. Serious coffee lovers head for **Cafés Verlet** in the 1st for beans from Rwanda, or **Brûlerie des Gobelins** in the 5th for its celebrated house blend.

04

Chocolate box

For Parisians, chocolate is not an everyday indulgence but a pleasure to be taken seriously. Modern chocolate shops, such as **La Maison du Chocolat** in the 8th and **Jean-Paul Hévin** in the 1st, look like boutiques full of jewels and the goods are only slightly less expensive. **A l'Etoile d'Or** in the 9th, run by Denise Acabo, has a selection from the best chocolate-makers around France, such as Bernachon and Dufoux. Other excellent shops are **Michel Chaudun** and **Debauve et Gallais**, both in the 7th.

Legendary food halls

Dalloyau Galeries gourmandes
Palais des Congrès
2 pl Porte Maillot, 17th
Ⓜ Porte-Maillot
Ⓣ 01 40 68 10 04
dalloyau.fr
⊕ 1/A4

Fauchon
26 pl de la Madeleine, 8th
Ⓜ Madeleine
Ⓣ 01 70 39 38 00
fauchon.fr
⊕ 6/K7

La Grande Epicerie du Bon Marché
38 r de Sèvres, 7th
Ⓜ Sèvres-Babylone
Ⓣ 01 44 39 81 00
lebonmarche.fr
⊕ 14/K14

Hédiard
21 pl de la Madeleine, 8th
Ⓜ Madeleine
Ⓣ 01 43 12 88 88
hediard.fr
⊕ 6/K7

Inno
31 r du Départ, 14th
Ⓜ Montparnasse-Bienvenüe
Ⓣ 01 43 20 69 30
monoprix.fr
⊕ 14/K16

Lafayette Gourmet
97 r de Provence, 9th
Ⓜ Havre Caumartin
Ⓣ 01 42 81 25 61
galerieslafayette.com
⊕ 2-6/L5

Gourmet grocers

Appellations d'Origine
26 r Lepic, 18th
Ⓜ Blanche
Ⓣ 01 42 62 94 66
⊕ 2/M2

Beau et Bon
81 r Lecourbe, 15th
Ⓜ Volontaires
Ⓣ 01 43 06 06 53
beauetbon.free.fr
⊕ 13/D17

Be Boulangépicier
73 bd Courcelles, 8th
Ⓜ Ternes
Ⓣ 01 46 22 20 20
alain-ducasse.com
⊕ 1-2/G3

Le Comptoir Colonial
22 r Lepic, 18th
Ⓜ Blanche
Ⓣ 01 42 58 44 84
lecomptoircolonial.com
⊕ 2/M2

Da Rosa
62 r de Seine, 6th
Ⓜ Mabillon
Ⓣ 01 45 21 41 30
restaurant-da-rosa.com
⊕ 11/N12

L'Epicerie
51 r St-Louis-en-l'Ile, 4th
Ⓜ Pont Marie
Ⓣ 01 43 25 20 14
⊕ 11/S13

Epicerie Fine Rive Gauche
8 r du Champ de Mars, 7th
Ⓜ École Militaire
Ⓣ 01 47 05 98 18
epiceriefinerivegauche.com
⊕ 9/F12

Granterroirs
30 r de Miromesnil, 8th
Ⓜ Miromesnil
Ⓣ 01 47 42 18 18
granterroirs.com
⊕ 6/I6

Aux Pipalottes Gourmandes
49 r de Rochechouart, 9th
Ⓜ Poissonnière
Ⓣ 01 44 53 04 53
⊕ 3/P3

Luxury foods

Bellota Bellota
18 r Jean Nicot, 7th
Ⓜ La Tour-Maubourg
ⓒ 01 53 59 96 96
✛ 9-10/G10

Comptoir Corrézien
8 r des Volontaires, 15th
Ⓜ Volontaires
ⓒ 01 47 83 52 97
✛ 13-14/G17

Comptoir de la Gastronomie
34 r Montmartre, 1st
Ⓜ Les Halles
ⓒ 01 42 33 31 32
comptoir-gastronomie.com
✛ 10/H10

Comptoirs de la Tour d'Argent
2 r du Cardinal Lemoine, 5th
Ⓜ Cardinal Lemoine
ⓒ 01 46 33 45 58
✛ 15/R14

Ducs de Gascogne
111 r St Antoine, 4th
ⓒ 01 42 71 17 72
Ⓜ Saint-Paul
ducsdegascogne.com
✛ 11-12/T12

Foie Gras de Luxe
26 r Montmartre, 1st
Ⓜ Les Halles
ⓒ 01 42 33 28 15
✛ 7/P8

Labeyrie
11 r d'Auteuil, 16th
Ⓜ Église d'Auteuil
ⓒ 01 42 24 17 62
labeyrie.fr
✛ Off map

Lafitte
8 r Jean du Bellay, 4th
Ⓜ Pont Marie
ⓒ 01 43 26 08 63
lafitte.fr
✛ 11/R13

La Maison de la Truffe
19 pl de la Madeleine, 8th
Ⓜ Madeleine
ⓒ 01 42 65 53 22
maison-de-la-truffe.fr
✛ 6/K7

Petrossian
18 bd de La Tour-Maubourg, 7th
Ⓜ Invalides
ⓒ 01 44 11 32 22
petrossian.com
✛ 10/H10

Un Saumon à Paris
110 r Monge, 5th
Ⓜ Censier-Daubenton
ⓒ 01 43 36 78 25
✛ 15/R16

Terres de Truffes
21 r Vignon, 8th
Ⓜ Madeleine
ⓒ 01 53 43 80 44
terresdetruffes.com
✛ 6/K6

04

Oils, honeys and condiments

A l'Olivier
23 r de Rivoli, 4th
Ⓜ Saint Paul
Ⓒ 01 48 04 86 59
alolivier.com
⊕ 11/S12

Maille
6 pl de la Madeleine, 8th
Ⓜ Madeleine
Ⓒ 01 40 15 06 00
maille.com
⊕ 6/K7

Produits des Monastères
10 r des Barres, 4th
Ⓜ Pont Marie
Ⓒ 01 48 04 39 05
⊕ 11/R12

Les Abeilles
21 r de la Butte aux Cailles,
13th
Ⓜ Corvisart
Ⓒ 01 45 81 43 48
lesabeilles.biz
⊕ Off map

La Maison du Miel
24 r Vignon, 9th
Ⓜ Madeleine
Ⓒ 01 47 42 26 70
maisondumiel.com
⊕ 6/K6

Les Ruchers du Roy
37 r du Roi de Sicile, 4th
Ⓜ Saint Paul
Ⓒ 01 42 72 02 96
lesruchersduroy.com
⊕ 11/S12

Huilerie Leblanc
6 r Jacob, 6th
Ⓜ Mabillon
Ⓒ 01 46 34 61 55
huile-leblanc.com
⊕ 10/M12

Oliviers & Co.
28 r de Buci, 6th
Ⓜ St-Germain-des-Prés
Ⓒ 01 44 07 15 43
oliviers-co.com
⊕ 11/N12

Sur les Quais
Marché d'Aligre, 12th
Ⓜ Faidherbe-Chaligny
Ⓒ 01 43 43 21 09
⊕ 12-16/X14

Spices, teas and coffees

Brûlerie des Gobelins
2 av des Gobelins, 5th
Ⓜ Les Gobelins
Ⓒ 01 43 31 90 13
⊕ 15/Q17

Cafés Amazone
11 r Rambuteau, 4th
Ⓜ Rambuteau
Ⓒ 01 48 87 20 90
⊕ 11/R10

Les Comptoirs Richard
73 r Lecourbe, 15th
Ⓜ Sèvres Lecourbe
Ⓒ 01 40 65 20 07
richard.fr
⊕ 13/F16

**La Brûlerie de
Montmartre**
66 r Damrémont, 18th
Ⓜ Lamarck-
Caulaincourt
Ⓒ 01 42 54 26 29
⊕ Off map

Cafés Verlet
256 r St Honoré, 1st
Ⓜ Palais Royal
Ⓒ 01 42 60 67 39
cafesverlet.com
⊕ 6/M9

Les Contes de Thé
60 r du Cherche Midi,
6th
Ⓜ Saint-Placide
Ⓒ 01 45 49 45 96
⊕ 14/K15

Goumanyat et son Royaume
3 r Charles François Dupuis, 3rd
Ⓜ République
Ⓣ 01 44 78 96 74
goumanyat.com
✛ 7 8/T8

Izraël
30 r François Miron, 4th
Ⓜ Saint-Paul
Ⓣ 01 42 72 66 23
✛ 11/S12

Chocolate box

A l'Etoile d'Or/ Denise Acabo
30 r Fontaine, 9th
Ⓜ Blanche
Ⓣ 01 48 74 59 55
✛ 2/M2

A la Reine Astrid
24 r du Cherche Midi , 6th
Ⓜ Saint-Placide
Ⓣ 01 42 84 07 02
✛ 14/K15

Debauve et Gallais
30 r des Sts-Pères, 7th
Ⓜ St-Germain-des-Prés
Ⓣ 01 45 48 54 67
debauve-et-gallais.com
✛ 10/M11

Lapeyronie
3 r Brantôme, 3rd
Ⓜ Rambuteau
Ⓣ 01 40 27 97 57
lapeyronie.fr
✛ 11/R10

La Maison des Trois Thés
1 r St Médard, 5th
Ⓜ Place Monge
Ⓣ 01 43 36 93 84
✛ 15/Q16

Jean-Charles Rochoux
16 r d'Assas, 6th
Ⓜ Rennes
Ⓣ 01 42 84 29 54
✛ 14/I14

Jean-Paul Hévin
231 r St Honoré, 1st
Ⓜ Tuileries
Ⓣ 01 55 35 35 96
jphevin.com
✛ 6/M9

La Maison du Chocolat
225 r du Fbg St-Honoré, 8th
Ⓜ Ternes
Ⓣ 01 42 27 39 44
lamaisonduchocolat.com
✛ 1-5/F5

Mariage Frères
30 r du Bourg Tibourg, 4th
Ⓜ Hôtel de Ville
Ⓣ 01 42 72 28 11
mariagefreres.com
✛ 11/R11

Le Palais des Thés
64 r Vieille-du-Temple, 3rd
Ⓜ Saint-Paul
Ⓣ 01 48 87 80 60
palaisdesthes.com
✛ 11/S11

04

Michel Chaudun
149 r de l'Université, 7th
Ⓜ Invalides
Ⓣ 01 47 53 74 40
✛ 10/K11

Patrick Roger
108 bd St Germain, 6th
Ⓜ Cluny La Sorbonne
Ⓣ 01 43 29 38 42
patrickroger.com
✛ 11/13

See page 9 to scan the directory

FRESH PICKS
AND MARKET STALLS

Mârché d'Aligre
Rue d'Aligre, 12th

I n a city where locals think nothing of queueing at the bakery twice a day for bread straight from the oven, it's no surprise that freshness is something of an obsession. If supermarkets have become a necessity for those with long work days, the sensual pleasure of buying from open-air food markets and specialist food shops is appreciated. It's also a more human way of doing business: good sales assistants get to know their regulars' tastes over time and set aside the creamiest goat's cheese or choicest fish for their preferred customers. Queues move slowly at neighbourhood markets as stallholders and their customers exchange health complaints and gossip, but nobody seems to mind. shopping in this unhurried way is what makes Paris feel like a village.

Markets

Paris has 82 food markets, about four for each *arrondissement*, though they aren't evenly distributed. Most are roving markets, which set up two or three times a week along a broad boulevard or in a square and operate from 8am to 2pm (and occasionally in the late afternoon), before disappearing in a flurry of green cleaning trucks. Roving markets can be tiny, like

05

the one on **place Maubert** in the Latin Quarter, or huge like the **Bastille** market, which starts at place de la Bastille and runs the length of boulevard Richard Lenoir. It might come as a surprise that only about ten percent of the stallholders are farmers selling food they have grown; most vendors stock up at the wholesale market in Rungis outside Paris before dawn. To spot the small producers, look for those with more rustic, seasonal wares and the sign *producteur* or *maraîcher* at the back of the stall. Markets are busiest on weekends, when locals stock up on fresh foods, and tend to be less frenetic during the week.

There are also 13 covered markets, housed in historic market halls and operating daily, except Mondays and Sunday afternoons. These include the restored **Enfants-Rouges** market on rue de Bretagne in the 3rd, originally dating from 1615. Unlike stallholders at many of the other markets, those here sell hot dishes to eat at tables on the premises, so you can enjoy the market experience to the full, even if you don't feel like cooking.

Each market reflects the personality of its neighbourhood. **Aligre**, in the 12th, is brash and boisterous along rue d'Aligre, with the best produce towards the Beauvau covered market on place d'Aligre. The atmosphere grows calm inside the market hall, where top-quality cheese shops Philippe Langlet and Pommier, and butcher Michel Brunon, cater to this up-and-coming area's bobos (*bourgeois-bohèmes*).

Saxe-Breteuil along the avenue de Saxe is probably the city's most polite and sedate market, catering to the aristocratic residents of the 7th *arrondissement*. The left-hand aisle, if you're facing the Eiffel Tower, is a kind of Park Avenue of produce. Look in particular for a stand stocked with apples of all kinds, including some English varieties that turn out to be perfectly suited to French pastries.

Just as chic, but a little more brash, is the **Président Wilson** market near Trocadéro in the 16th. Though the quality is uniformly high, the main attraction is star market gardener Joël Thiébault, who grows 1,600 vegetable varieties at his farm outside Paris. Chefs such as Pascal Barbot at Astrance can't get enough of Thiébault's multicoloured carrots, Thai herbs, yellow-ribbed chard and pink-and-white striped beetroot.

The **rue Lepic** street market retains an old Montmartre feel. The **Boucherie des Gourmets**, run by Robert Debeaux, offers no-additive products only and is well known for its terrines, pâtés, and meat sourced from small farms in southwest France.

05

Boucherie de la Place des Vosges
3 rue du Pas-de-la-Mule, 4th

Specialist shops

Although you can buy everything you need in a good open-air market, from a deboned and stuffed guinea hen to individually wrapped tropical fruits, the variety of meat, fish, cheese and bread is rarely as good as in specialist shops. Only a real shortage of time and money pushes a Parisian to buy packaged meat – each neighbourhood has its butchers and *charcutiers* who take enormous pride in their work. Chickens are displayed with their head and feet on, to show what breed of bird you are buying and prove that it was free-range (only free-range chickens develop claws). The butcher will ask what dish you are preparing so as to cut and trim the meat correctly, and even minced beef will be prepared before your eyes so that you know it is fresh.

05

Butchers and charcuteries

Down a side street in quartier Daguerre in the 14th, **Hugo Desnoyer** is the butcher that chefs such as Pierre Gagnaire and Bernard Pacaud of l'Ambroisie turn to for the finest French meats: limousine, Aubrac and Salers beef, alongside Lozère lamb that has fed on wild herbs. Even more discreetly located is **Joël Meurdesoif**, whose acclaimed charcuterie is hidden within the courtyard of a modern building a few blocks away from the Paris Chinatown. Meurdesoif (whose name, appropriately, means "dying of thirst") supplies his melt-in-the-mouth pâtés to a number of the city's best wine bars. With a prestigious Ile St-Louis location, **Jean-Paul Gardil** has what is probably the most artful window display of any Paris butcher, complete with plaques showing the awards his suppliers have won. The butcher shop **Alain Tribolet** on rue Montorgeuil market street in the 2nd is more than 100 years old – and his beef is beautifully aged, too. More unusual these days are *volaillers*, shops devoted to poultry; one that remains is **Le Coq Saint-Honoré** in the 1st, where you'll find rare breeds of chicken, and pigeon from the Vendée region.

Fishmongers

If nothing can quite beat downing oysters by the sea, Paris is close enough to Normandy and Brittany for the best fishmongers to be able to sell you that morning's catch. Fish doesn't come any fresher in Paris than at **La Poissonnerie du Dôme**, next to the celebrated Montparnasse fish restaurant Le Dôme. Jean-Pierre Lopez, the owner since 1987, hand-selects small quantities of line-caught fish directly from the boats just after midnight, and by 8 the next morning his staff has displayed the day's finds. The fish are never piled on top of each other, even during transport, nor do they ever come into direct contact with ice. Another excellent fishmonger is **Poissonnerie Sablaise** on the rue Cler market street in the 7th, where the fish and seafood are remarkably fresh and staff are efficient and friendly. High-quality fish comes at a considerable cost in Paris, but l'**Océanic**, in the Les Halles district, sells its fish to the public at near-wholesale prices on Saturday mornings only from 8am to noon.

Greengrocers

Parisians who don't have time to visit the markets on weekday mornings are grateful for the fresh fruit and vegetable shops known as *primeurs*, the best of which hand-pick the finest produce from France and elsewhere at the wholesale market Rungis. *Primeurs* vary in quality, but one of the best is **Opéra Primeurs**, whose potatoes and salad greens are the next best thing to having your own garden. **Jardin du Marais**, among the food shops of rue de Bretagne, also has exemplary produce and irresistible wild mushrooms in season.

Cheesemongers

A *crèmerie* sells dairy products, including cheese, while a true *fromagerie* ages its cheeses in cellars on the premises, enabling them to be sold at the peak of ripeness. Of the many shops claiming to be *fromageries* in Paris, only a dozen or so have their own cellars. Marie Quatrehomme married into a family of *fromagers* but her passion for cheese is evident from the moment you enter her shop, **Quatrehomme** on rue de Sèvres,

05

Marché Bastille
Boulevard Richard Lenoir, 11th

where 34-month-old Comté sourced near the Swiss border is displayed by the entrance next to a poster of different breeds of milk cows. To remind people that the first French cheeses were made by monks, she stocks monastery cheeses such as a creamy, oval goat's cheese from the Pyrénées.

Josiane Molard, whose little boutique **Fromagerie Molard** on rue des Martyrs in the 9th could easily go unnoticed, also shares a penchant for cheeses from monasteries and very small producers. Another member of the cheese sisterhood is **Marie-Anne Cantin** in the 7th, who supplies many of the city's top chefs. One of the leading men in the cheese business is Philippe Alléosse, who ages 150 to 200 different cheeses in his spacious **Alléosse** cellars on rue Poncelet in the 17th. The small chain of cheese shops **Androuët**, founded by Henri Androuët in 1909, has maintained its high quality, with particularly helpful staff. In the quartier Daguerre, **Fromage Rouge** offers high-quality cheeses matured on site.

Bakers

Though it's easy to take great bread for granted, there has been a mini-revolution in breadmaking over the past 20 years. Passionate bakers promoted traditional methods in a backlash against time-saving industrial

Organic sources

Go to the **Raspail** organic market on a Sunday morning and you may run into local celebrities such as Catherine Deneuve or television cook Ina Garten in rustic mode. If the Raspail market and its Right Bank equivalent along **boulevard des Batignolles** have long had a following, the organic movement has been dusting off its image in the past few years. Clean and bright organic supermarkets including the **Naturalia** chain have been opening all over Paris. Many bakeries, including **Pain Michel Moisan** and **Bread & Roses**, use organic flour for better flavour and texture rather than to make a political statement. Big organic supermarkets such as **Canal Bio** and **Les Nouveaux Robinson,** in the Paris suburbs of Boulogne, Montreuil and Neuilly, sell everything from organic meat to wine, making it possible to eat 100 per cent organic for those who can afford it.

To find organic foods in ordinary supermarkets, look for the AB (Agriculture Biologique) label.

techniques that resulted in fluffy, tasteless baguettes and a dramatic drop in French bread consumption. The new star of French bread and viennoiseries, Christophe Vasseur, opened his first shop, **Du Pain et des Idées**, near République, and has set up another one near Châtelet.

Pastry shops

The number of pastry shops in Paris can seem astounding for those to whom cake is an occasional treat. Keep in mind that the French rarely indulge in industrial chocolate bars, preferring to treat themselves to a decadent *gâteau*. Bread and pastry are separate arts, and bakers, with rare exceptions, excel at one or the other. The leading light of the Paris pastry scene is **Pierre Hermé**, known as the Picasso of pâtisserie. However, a few young pastry chefs, some of them trained by Hermé, have opened shops that rival his Saint-Germain boutique, among them Didier Mathray at **Pain de Sucre** in the Marais, and Claire Damon at **Des Gâteaux et du Pain** in the 15th.

05

Markets

Aligre
Tues and Sun
Pl d'Aligre, 12th
Ⓜ Ledru-Rollin
marchedaligre.free.fr
⊕ 16/X14

Enfants-Rouges
Tues and Sun
39 r de Bretagne, 3rd
Ⓜ Filles de Calvaire
⊕ 7/T9

Président Wilson
Wed and Sat
Av du Pdt Wilson, 16th
Ⓜ Iéna
⊕ 5/C9

Bastille
Thur and Sun
Bd Richard Lenoir, 11th
Ⓜ Bastille
⊕ 12V11

Lepic
Tues and Sun
R Lepic, 18th
Ⓜ Blanche
⊕ 2/M2

**Saint-Eustache –
Les Halles**
Thur and Sun
R Montmartre
Ⓜ Châtelet
⊕ 7/P8

Bourse
Tues and Fri
Pl de la Bourse
Ⓜ Bourse
⊕ 7/O7

Maubert
Tues, Thur and Sat
Pl Maubert, 5th
Ⓜ Maubert Mutualité
⊕ 15/Q14

Saxe-Breteuil
Thur and Sat
Av de Saxe, 7th
Ⓜ Ségur
Thur and Sat
⊕ 14/H14

Butchers and charcuteries

Alain Tribolet
54 r Montorgueil, 2nd
Ⓜ Etienne Marcel
Ⓒ 01 42 33 04 06
⊕ 7/P9

Boucherie Lamartine
172 av Victor Hugo, 16th
Ⓜ Victor Hugo
Ⓒ 01 47 27 82 29
⊕ 5/A7

Boucherie Pl des Vosges
3 r du Pas-de-la-Mule, 4th
Ⓜ Chemin Vert
Ⓒ 01 42 72 50 42
⊕ 12/U12

Boucherie des Gourmets
18 r Lepic,18th
Ⓜ Blanche
Ⓒ 01 42 55 82 87
⊕ 2/M2

Boucherie de la Mairie
41 r de Bretagne, 3rd
Ⓜ Filles de Calvaire
Ⓒ 01 48 87 90 12
⊕ 7-8/T9

Charcuterie Lyonnaise
58 r des Martyrs, 9th
Ⓜ Pigalle
Ⓒ 01 48 78 96 45
⊕ 3/O2

Le Coq Saint-Honoré
3 r Gomboust, 1st
Ⓜ Pyramides
Ⓒ 01 42 61 53 30
coqsthonore.fr
⊕ 6/M8

Gilles Vérot
7 r Lecourbe, 15th
Ⓜ Sèvres Lecourbe
Ⓒ 01 47 34 01 03
⊕ 13/F16

Le Lann
242 bis r des Pyrénées, 20th
Ⓜ Pelleport
Ⓒ 01 47 97 12 79
⊕ Off map

Aux Fleurons de la Viande
59 r Monge, 5th
Ⓜ Place Monge
Ⓒ 01 45 35 16 46
⊕ 15/R16

Jean-Paul Gardil
44 r St-Louis-en-l'Île, 4th
Ⓜ Pont Marie
Ⓒ 01 43 54 97 15
⊕ 11/S13

Michel Brunon
Marché couvert Beauvau,
Pl d'Aligre, 12th
Ⓜ Ledru-Rollin
Ⓒ 01 43 40 62 58
⊕ 16/X14

Gilles Vérot
7 r Lecourbe, 15th
Ⓜ Sèvres Lecourbe
Ⓒ 01 47 34 01 03
⊕ 13/F16

Joël Meurdesoif
8 r Albert Bayet, 13th
Ⓜ Place d'Italie
Ⓒ 01 42 16 81 83
⊕ Off map

Les Viandes du Champs de Mars
122 r St Dominique, 7th
Ⓜ Ecole Militaire
Ⓒ 01 47 05 53 52
⊕ 9/F11

05

Fishmongers

L'Écume St-Honoré
6 pl du Marché
St Honoré, 1st
Ⓜ Tuileries
Ⓒ 01 42 61 93 87
⊕ 6/M8

Pepone
65 r des Abbesses, 18th
Ⓜ Abbesses
Ⓒ 01 42 64 29 94
⊕ 3/N1

La Poissonnerie du Dôme
4 r Delambre, 14th
Ⓜ Vavin
Ⓒ 01 43 35 23 95
poissonneriedudome.com
⊕ 14/L17

L'Océanic
39 r Étienne Marcel, 1st
Ⓜ Étienne Marcel
Ⓒ 01 42 36 22 37
loceanic.com
⊕ 7/P9

Poissonnerie du Bac
69 r du Bac, 7th
Ⓜ Rue du Bac
Ⓒ 01 45 48 06 64
⊕ 10/K12

Poissonnerie Sablaise
28 r Cler, 7th
Ⓜ École Militaire
Ⓒ 01 45 51 61 78
⊕ 9-10/G11

Greengrocers

**Aux Beaux Fruits
de France**
304 r St Honoré, 1st
Ⓜ Tuileries
Ⓣ 01 42 60 45 26
⊕ 6/M9

Jardin du Marais
29 r de Bretagne, 3rd
Ⓜ Filles du Calvaire
Ⓣ 01 42 72 61 02
⊕ 7-8/T9

Opéra Primeurs
21 r Danielle Casanova, 1st
Ⓜ Opéra
Ⓣ 01 42 28 60 05.
⊕ 6/M8

Cheesemongers

Alléosse
13 r Poncelet 17th
Ⓜ Ternes
Ⓣ 01 46 22 50 45
fromage-alleosse.com
⊕ 1/E3

Fromage Rouge
19 r Daguerre, 14th
Ⓜ Denfert-Rochereau
Ⓣ 01 43 21 19 09
⊕ Off map

Philippe Langlet
Marché couvert Beauvau
Pl d'Aligre, 12th
Ⓜ Ledru-Rollin
Ⓣ 01 43 45 35 09
⊕ 12-16/X14

Androuët
93 r Cambronne, 15th
Ⓜ Vaugirard
Ⓣ 01 47 83 32 05
androuet.com
⊕ 13/F16

Laurent Dubois
2 r Lourmel, 15th
Ⓜ Dupleix
Ⓣ 01 45 78 70 58
⊕ 13/C14

Quatrehomme
62 r de Sèvres, 7th
Ⓜ Vaneau
Ⓣ 01 47 34 33 45
⊕ 14/J14

Fromagerie Boursault
71 av du Gl Leclerc, 14th
Ⓜ Alésia
Ⓣ 01 45 38 59 56
⊕ Off map

Marie-Anne Cantin
12 r du Champs de Mars, 7th
Ⓜ École Militaire
Ⓣ 01 45 50 43 94
cantin.fr
⊕ 9/F12

Ronalba
54 r du Fbg St-Denis,
10th
Ⓜ Château d'Eau
Ⓣ 01 44 83 96 30
⊕ 7/R6

Fromagerie Molard
48 r des Martyrs, 9th
Ⓜ Saint-Georges
Ⓣ 01 45 26 84 88
⊕ 3/O3

Marie-Bocquet
32 r des Abbesses, 18th
Ⓜ 01 42 52 96 27
⊕ 3/N1

Le Savoyard
39 r Popincourt, 10th
Ⓜ St-Ambroise
Ⓣ 01 43 55 48 63
⊕ 12/W11

Bakers

Arnaud Delmontel
39 r des Martyrs, 9th
Ⓜ Saint-Georges
Ⓒ 01 48 78 29 33
arnaud-delmontel.com
⊕ 3/O4

L'Autre Boulange
43 r de Montreuil, 11th
Ⓜ Faidherbe Chaligny
Ⓒ 01 43 72 86 04
lautreboulange.com
⊕ 16/Z14

Bread & Roses
62 r Madame, 6th
Ⓜ St Sulpice
Ⓒ 01 42 22 06 06
⊕ 14/M14

Eric Kayser
8 r Monge, 5th
Ⓜ Maubert Mutualité
Ⓒ 01 44 07 01 42
maison-kayser.com
⊕ 15/Q14

Gosselin
125 r St Honoré, 1st
Ⓜ Louvre Rivoli
Ⓒ 01 45 08 03 59
boulangerie-gosselin.com
⊕ 11/O10

Le Grenier à Pain
38 r des Abbesses, 18th
Ⓜ Abbesses
Ⓒ 01 46 06 41 81
⊕ 3/N1

Julien
75 r St Honoré, 1st
Ⓜ Pont Neuf
Ⓒ 01 42 36 24 83
maisonjulien.fr
⊕ 11/O10

Du Pain et des idées
34 r Yves Toudic, 10th
Ⓜ Jacques Bonsergent
Ⓒ 01 42 40 44 52
⊕ 7-8/T6

Poilâne
8 r du Cherche Midi, 6th
Ⓜ Saint-Sulpice
Ⓒ 01 44 39 26 50
poilane.fr
⊕ 10/L13

05

Organic sources

Batignolles market
Sat
Bd de Batignolles, 8th
Ⓜ Rome
⊕ 2/K2

Biocoop Paris Glacière
55 r de la Glacière, 13th
Ⓜ Glacière
Ⓒ 01 45 35 24 36
⊕ Off map

Le Boulanger de Monge
123 r Monge, 5th
Ⓜ Censier Daubenton
Ⓒ 01 43 37 54 20
leboulangerdemonge.com
⊕ 15/Q17

Bread & Roses
7 r de Fleurus, 6th
Ⓜ Saint-Placide
Ⓒ 01 42 22 06 06
breadandroses.fr
⊕ 14/M15

Cibus
5 r Molière, 1st
Ⓜ Palais-Royal
Ⓒ 01 42 61 50 19
⊕ 7/N8

Canal Bio
300 r de Charenton, 12th
Ⓜ Dugommier
Ⓒ 01 44 73 81 50
canalbio.club.fr
⊕ 16/Y16

Organic sources suite

Dietetic shop
11 r Delambre, 14th
Ⓜ Vavin
Ⓒ 01 43 35 39 75
dietetic-shop.fr
⊕ 14/L17

Kayser Bio
14 r Monge, 5th
Ⓜ Maubert Mutualité
Ⓒ 01 44 07 17 81
maison-kayser.com
⊕ 11-15/Q14

Naturalia
11-13 r Montorgueil, 1st
Ⓜ Les Halles
Ⓒ 01 55 80 77 81
naturalia.fr
⊕ 7/P8

Les Nouveaux Robinson
49 r Raspail, 93100
Montreuil-sous-Bois
Ⓜ Robespierre
Ⓒ 01 49 88 70 44
nouveauxrobinson.fr
⊕ Off map

Pain Michel Moisan
5 pl d'Aligre, 12th
Ⓜ Ledru Rollin
Ⓒ 01 43 45 46 60
⊕ 16/X14

Planète Bio
30 bd St Germain, 5th
Ⓜ Maubert Mutualité
Ⓒ 01 44 07 34 84
⊕ 15/R14

Raspail market
Sun
Bd Raspail, 6th
Ⓜ Rennes
⊕14/L15

Rendez-Vous Nature
96 r Mouffetard, 5th
Ⓜ Censier Daubenton
Ⓒ 01 43 36 59 34
dietetiquemouffetard.com
⊕ 15/Q17

Rose Bakery
46 r des Martyrs, 9th
Ⓜ Notre-Dame-de-Lorette
Ⓒ 01 42 82 12 80
⊕ 3/O4

Saint Charles market
Tue, Fri
R St Charles, 15th
Ⓜ Charles Michels
⊕ 13/A16

Wada
19 r de l'Arc de Triomphe, 17th
Ⓜ Ternes
Ⓒ 01 44 09 79 19
⊕ 1/D4

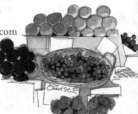

Pastry shops

Arnaud Larher
53 r Caulaincourt, 18th
Ⓜ Lamarck Caulaincourt
Ⓒ 01 42 57 68 08
arnaud-larher.com
⊕ 2/M1

La Bague de Kenza
106 r St Maur, 11th
Ⓜ Rue Saint-Maur
Ⓒ 01 43 14 93 15
labaguedekenza.com
⊕ 8/W8

Bonbonnière de Buci
12 r de Buci, 6th
Ⓜ Mabillon
Ⓒ 01 43 26 97 13
⊕ 11/N12

Des Gâteaux et du Pain
63 bd Pasteur, 15th
Ⓜ Pasteur
Ⓒ 01 45 38 94 16
⊕ 14/H16

Gérard Mulot
76 r de Seine, 6th
Ⓜ Odéon
Ⓒ 01 43 26 85 77
gerard-mulot.com
⊕ 11/N12

Jean-Paul Hévin
231 r St Honoré, 1st
Ⓜ Tuileries
Ⓒ 01 55 35 35 96
jphevin.com
⊕ 6/M9

Ladurée
75 av des Champs-
Élysées, 8th
Ⓜ Franklin D. Roosevelt
Ⓒ 01 40 75 08 75
laduree.fr
⊕ 5/F6

Du Pain et des Idées
24 r St Martin, 4th
Ⓜ Hôtel de Ville
Ⓒ 01 48 87 46 17
⊕ 7/R9

Pain de Sucre
14 r Rambuteau, 3rd
Ⓜ Rambuteau
Ⓒ 01 45 74 68 92
⊕ 11/R10

Les Petits Mitrons
26 r Lepic, 18th
Ⓜ Blanche
Ⓒ 01 46 06 10 29
lespetitsmitrons.com
⊕ 2/M2

Pierre Hermé
72 r Bonaparte, 6th
Ⓜ St-Germain-des-Prés
Ⓒ 01 43 54 47 77
pierreherme.com
⊕ 10/M13

Sadaharu Aoki
35 r de Vaugirard, 6th
Ⓜ Saint-Placide
Ⓒ 01 45 44 48 90
sadaharuaoki.com
⊕ 14/K15

05

See page 9
to scan the
directory

THE FAST TRACK
TO FINE WINES

Legrand Filles et Fils
1 rue de la Banque, 2nd, galerie Vivienne

Previous page: La Crèmerie
9 rue des Quatre-Vents, 6th

When it comes to French wines, it makes sense to explore the huge variety available, particularly from regions such as the South West, Languedoc, Alsace, Corsica and the Jura, which have been working hard to compete in the world market. Of course, if it's vintage Bordeaux you're after, there are plenty of places to find that too, from wine chain stores such as Nicolas to the cellar at the Plaza Athénée.

Unmissable wine shops

Ub

One of the great pleasures of Paris life is selecting just the right bottle with the help of a *caviste* (wine shop owner). One of the oldest and best-stocked wine shops in Paris is **Caves Augé,** in the 8th, which focuses on natural wines (hand-harvested, often unfiltered, with minimal or no chemical products and sulphites) and arranges free tastings with wine growers.

Another classic is **Au Verger de la Madeleine**, with its old-fashioned façade and jaw-dropping selection of rare bottles. This is the place to come to for a 1961 Pétrus or a 1971 Romanée Conti, if you can spend up to €15,000 for a single bottle.

Equally serious about its wines is **Les Caves Taillevent**, set up by Taillevent restaurant owner Jean-Claude Vrinat in the 8th. The cellars of this sleek modern shop house some 1,400 wines, just a sample of the many thousands of bottles that are stored in the restaurant's main cellar outside Paris. You can choose bottles under €10 from its Cave du Jour, and there are free tastings on Saturdays.

L'Atelier de Joël Robuchon also has its own *cave* close to the restaurant in the 7th. Another remarkable restaurant *cave,* run by the owners of Fish, is **La Dernière Goutte** in the 6th. Here you can attend free tastings with visiting winemakers on Saturdays. **La Cave du Square Trousseau,** linked to a popular bistro in the 12th only a few steps from Marché d'Aligre, has one of the best selections of fashionable wines. Just as forward-thinking is the wine emporium **Lavinia,** near the Madeleine, with its selection of 6,000 wines and spirits, 2,000 of which are international. Most French wine regions are well represented. In the restaurant upstairs, the wines are sold at the same price as those in the shop.

No wine connoisseur's tour of Paris would be complete without a visit to the charming **Legrand Filles et Fils**, in the 19th-century covered passage of Galerie Vivienne across from Palais-Royal in the 2nd. Tastings here are by reservation.

Small and exclusive

Some smaller wine shops attract a loyal clientele because of the unique expertise of their owners. The
winner here (often quoted by his fellow *cavistes*) is
Francis Bessette at **Caves du Château**, who manages to
spend time in vineyards to increase his already considerable knowledge about the wines sold in his dusty
shop in Vincennes. The advice of Raphaël Gimenez at
Les Caprices de l'Instant near Bastille in the 4th is also
greatly appreciated. He will provide a personal, written
prescription for each bottle, including details on the time
for decanting and the dishes that best go with the wine.

Young but very experienced, Nicolas Julhès runs
Ronalba, a wine and cheese shop in the 10th. Julhès,
also a consultant on wine and whisky for LVMH, loves
to help clients find a bottle that exactly fits their needs.
De Vinis, Lionel Michelin's wine shop in the 5th, focuses on very old vintages. **Vins Rares Peter Thustrup**,
in the 16th, will look for vintage gems at a minimum
price of €1,500 for private clients, although he mainly
works with wine professionals.

Ancient vintages can be found at bargain prices at
wine and cheese shop **Le Savoyard**, on rue Popincourt
near Eglise Saint Ambroise in the 10th. An excellent
choice is also available at **Caves du Panthéon**, near the

06

L'Atelier de Joël Robuchon
5 rue de Montalembert, 7th

Jardin du Luxembourg and **Cavestève**, near Bastille in the 4th, with a bright modern design. The Paris specialist in Languedoc wines, **Les Crus du Soleil**, near Montparnasse, has frequent tastings accompanied by Languedoc charcuterie à la carte. For a wide range of prestigious vintages from Bordeaux go to **La Maison des Millésimes** in Saint-Germain-des-Prés in the 6th.

Flashy names and chains

Around place de la Madeleine, three upscale shops compete for wine lovers: **Hédiard**, **Fauchon** and **Nicolas** keep prestigious wines such as Romanée Conti. One of the most recent *caves* is **Caves Bernard Magrez** on rue Saint Augustin not far from Lafayette Gourmet. Magrez sells the fashionable wines made by his business partner Gérard Depardieu, and has built a wine empire including prestigious Bordeaux *grands crus* as well as cheaper, but well-marketed wines.

Out-of-town bargains

If you have time, it's worth making a special trip outside the city to one of the two warehouses of **Châteaux Cash and Carry**, either in Saint-Denis, north of Paris, or Malakoff, south of Paris. Owned by a Bordeaux family, these stores stock an incredible array of well-known names at reduced prices (sometimes half what you would pay at previously mentioned shops).

Organic options

A few wine cellars are focusing on natural, organic and biodynamic wines, which customers have got to know by tasting them in Paris wine bars. Part wine shop and part antique store, **La Cave de l'Insolite** stocks wines from natural producers. **L'Estaminet Arômes et Cépages**, in the Marché des Enfants Rouges, also focuses on natural wines.

La Cave des Papilles, near rue Daguerre – not to be confused with the wine bar **Les Papilles** *(see page 110)*, where you will also find natural wine – makes a point of seeking out up-and-coming natural producers, whose bottles are displayed alongside more familiar names such as the excellent Gramenon in the Côtes du Rhône.

Also worth a visit outside Paris is **Les Caves de Marly** near Versailles, owned by Alain Dutournier. The star chef keeps his restaurants' stock and bottles for private clients here, in an environment where they mature perfectly. Around a million bottles are stored in the cellars.

The best wine bars

One of the first wine bars to promote organic wines was **Le Verre Volé** on rue de Lancry in the 10th, which serves hearty food and also has a wine shop. Even tinier, **La Crèmerie** in the 6th also pairs natural wines with simple but top-quality products such as Spanish ham and Italian *burratta* cheese. **Les Fines Gueules**, Arnaud Bradol's wine bar on rue de la Vrillière in the 1st, has a similar concept. Bradol, with partner Alexandre Mathieu, is also behind **Le Bistral** *(see page 35)*, a restaurant very strong on wines on rue Lemercier in the 17th.

06

Wine bars can be among the most buzzing places in Paris for a night out, as is proven at the happening **La Muse Vin** east of Bastille, **Autour d'un Verre** near the Folies Bergères, or **Le Café de la Nouvelle Mairie** behind the Panthéon, facing Universal Music.

Despite imitators, the wine bar of choice for winemakers when they visit Paris remains **Le Baratin**, high up

Les Papilles
30 rue Gay Lussac, 5th

in Belleville, where Argentinean cook Raquel Carena and organic wine expert Philippe 'Pinuche' Pinoteau make a winning pair. Also popular with natural wine lovers is neighbour **Le Chapeau Melon**, run by former Baratin associate Olivier Camus.

The more sophisticated **Le Café du Passage**, on rue de Charonne in the shadows of Bastille, is perfect for a quiet evening. On weekends, it is a favourite spot for some of the sommeliers of fine restaurants, including Taillevent's Canadian Marco Pelletier. Another veteran wine bar is **Juvénile's** on rue des Petits Champs, well known for its impeccable selection of affordable wines and its truculent Scottish owner, Tim Johnston. At the wine bar **Les Enfants Rouges**, near the eponymous market, Dany Denis-Bertin, another wine bar legend, continues to serve great wines. For Bordeaux aficionados, no one beats **Le Petit Verdot**, on the lower end of rue du Cherche-Midi near the Tour Montparnasse. Here Ideya Ishizuka, the friendly Japanese sommelier, formerly at Cordeillan-Bages, near Bordeaux, serves a good selection of *crus* with decent cuisine.

Restaurants and sommeliers

High-end restaurants all take pride in their cellars and usually benefit from the expertise of star sommeliers. This is the case at **La Tour d'Argent**, where David

Late-night wine shopping

Most wine shops close at 8pm, and it is easy to find yourself high and dry with no bottle to take to a party, or suddenly faced with an empty cellar. Small corner grocery stores are infamous for stocking badly conserved wines and charging exorbitant prices, but there are some alternatives. **La Grande Epicerie** at Le Bon Marché department store with its excellent *cave à vins* is open until 9pm. Many larger branches of **Monoprix** stay open until 10pm (midnight on the Champs-Elysées); its **Daily Monop** stores are also open till midnight, though in certain areas they stop selling wine at 10pm. If you're near the Champs-Elysées you can visit **PublicisDrugstore**'s *cave à vins*, open till a very civilised 2am. Another cunning plan for sourcing a decent bottle late at night is to go to one of the wine bars that double as a wine shop, such as **Le Verre Volé** *(see page 99)*, or **Le Garde-Robe** near Les Halles – where you can even enjoy a leisurely dégustation with the owner while you choose.

Ridgeway manages one of the largest wine cellars in Paris. **L'Arpège** not only serves the best food for your money; its young sommeliers Guillaume Muller and Steve Jicquel provide friendly and knowledgeable advice on their wine list.

Fabulous wine lists can also be found at smaller and less well known restaurants such as **La Truffière** near the Panthéon, which boasts an incredible list of prestigious vintages of the great châteaux and domaines. **La Maison de l'Aubrac**, a meat specialist open all night on the south side of the Golden Triangle, has a good selection of wines, although no Bordeaux. Another meat specialist in the Montparnasse area, **Le Severo**, run by former butcher William Bernet, has reasonably priced wines selected by Marc Sibard, the dynamic manager of Caves Augé. Severo's neighbours **La Maison Courtine** and **A Mi-Chemin** also feature great wine lists. Unbeatable on fabulous bottles such as Romanée-Conti, **Le Villaret** serves an excellent cuisine near Oberkampf in the 11th.

In the 12th, **Le Trou Gascon**, an outstanding restaurant and the first venture of chef Alain Dutournier, serves food and wines from the South West and offers hundreds of Armagnacs, each with tasting notes. A good representative of another terroir of northeast

Ub

La Crèmerie
9 rue des Quatre Vents, 6th

France is Claude Steger, owner of **L'Alsaco** near Gare du Nord, who has a list of 400 Alsatian wines. You can take away bottles at the price you would pay if you bought them direct from the winery in Alsace.

Philippe Faure-Brac, a former Meilleur Sommelier du Monde (World's Best Sommelier), runs **Le Bistro du Sommelier** on boulevard Haussmann. Another award-winner, Olivier Poussier, manages the wine-list of **Elysées Lenôtre**, while master sommelier Eric Beaumard runs the total operation at **Le Cinq**.

A good place to taste wines from the Jura is **Maître Paul** near Odéon. For wines from Corsica, go to **Paris Main d'Or** in Bastille, which serves Corsican dishes with *charcuterie* sourced from the owner's village. Near the Opéra, **Drouant** has been given new life by the Alsatian chef Antoine Westermann. The selection is original, and each wine is available by the glass at the bar. A different winemaker presents his wines in the restaurant every Saturday. The most comprehensive list of Pomerol wines can be found in an unlikely place near the Musée d'Orsay: **Tan Dinh**, a Vietnamese restaurant whose managers, Robert and Freddy Vifian, are renowned for their knowledge of Pomerol. Two great restaurants for discovering well-priced fashionable wines from up-and-coming names are **Le Marsangy** in the 11th, and **l'Os à Moelle** in the 15th.

06

Wine courses and tastings

Master classes moderated by leading wine authorities such as Bernard Burtschy and Michel Bettane are offered in a cellar near the Panthéon by **Grains Nobles**. Prices vary from €85 to €150 per class. Also recommended for wine enthusiasts are monthly tastings (around €150 per session) under the leadership of master *caviste* Raphaël Gimenez at **Les Caprices de l'Instant,** his boutique near Bastille. **Lavinia** training sessions are designed for beginners, with prices from €30 to €50. At **O Chateau Wine Loft,** Olivier Magny offers classes in English, also for beginners.

If you are seeking a more in-depth introduction to French wines, consider the courses at **Legrand Filles et Fils**, **Cavestève** and **Le Jardin des Vignes**. Nothing beats learning among the vines themselves and **Les Vignes de Paris Bagatelle** offers this unique (for Paris) opportunity: you can sign up for an introductory or themed tasting course, and even learn to make your own wine at this vineyard in the Bois de Boulogne.

François Audouze puts on lavish wine dinners to share his passion for vintage wines. At €1,000 per guest, you may prefer simply to read about them on his blog www.academiedesvinsanciens.org.

Unmissable wine shops

**L'Atelier
Joël Robuchon**
5 r de Montalembert, 7th
Ⓜ Rue du Bac
ⓒ 01 42 22 56 56
⊕ 10/L11

**La Cave du Square
Trousseau**
1 r Antoine Vollon, 12th
Ⓜ Ledru-Rollin
ⓒ 01 43 43 06 00
⊕ 16/W14

Lavinia
3 bd de la Madeleine, 1st
Ⓜ Madeleine
ⓒ 01 42 97 20 20
lavinia.fr
⊕ 6/K7

Caves Augé
116 bd Haussmann, 8th
Ⓜ St Augustin
ⓒ 01 45 22 16 97
⊕ 2-6/J5

Les Caves Taillevent
199 r du Fbg
St-Honoré, 8th
Ⓜ Ternes
ⓒ 01 45 61 14 09
⊕ 1/F5

Legrand Filles et Fils
1 r de la Banque, 2nd
Ⓜ Bourse
ⓒ 01 42 60 07 12
caves-legrand.com
⊕ 7/O7

Caves Estève
10 r de la Cerisaie, 4th
Ⓜ Bastille
ⓒ 01 42 72 33 05
caveesteve.com
⊕ 12/U13

La Dernière Goutte
6 r de Bourbon
Le Château, 6th
Ⓜ St-Germain-des-Près
ⓒ 01 43 29 11 62
⊕ 11/N13

**Au Verger de
la Madeleine**
4 bd Malesherbes, 8th
Ⓜ Madeleine
ⓒ 01 42 65 51 99
verger-madeleine.com
⊕ 6/K7

06

Out-of-town bargains

Les Caves de Marly
29bis route de Versailles
Ⓜ Le Port Marly
ⓒ 01 39 17 04 00
⊕ Off map

**Châteaux Cash
and Carry**
166 av Pierre Brossolette,
Malakoff
Ⓜ Châtillon Montrouge
ⓒ 01 46 54 30 95
⊕ Off map

**Châteaux Cash
and Carry**
137 av Président Wilson,
Saint Denis
Ⓜ Porte de la Chapelle
ⓒ 01 55 93 40 90
⊕ Off map

Small and exclusive

**Les Caprices
de l'Instant**
12 r Jacques Coeur, 4th
Ⓜ Bastille
Ⓒ 01 40 27 89 00
⊕ 12/U13

Caves du Château
17 r Raymond du Temple,
Vincennes
Ⓡ Vincennes
Ⓒ 01 43 28 17 50
⊕ Off map

Caves du Panthéon
174 r St-Jacques, 5th
Ⓜ Maubert Mutualité
Ⓒ 01 46 33 90 35
⊕ 15/O15

Cavestève
10 r de la Cerisaie, 4th
Ⓜ Bastille
Ⓒ 01 42 72 33 05
cavesteve.com
⊕ 12/U13

Les Crus du Soleil
146 r du Château, 14th
Ⓜ Pernety
Ⓒ 01 45 39 78 99
⊕ Off map

De Vinis
48 r de la Montagne
Ste Geneviève, 5th
Ⓜ Maubert Mutualité
Ⓒ 01 43 36 12 12
devinis.fr
⊕ 15/Q15

Les Domaines qui Montent
136 bd Voltaire, 11th
Ⓜ Voltaire
Ⓒ 01 43 56 89 15
⊕ 12/Y12

La Maison des Millésimes
137 bd St Germain, 6th
Ⓜ Mabillon
Ⓒ 01 40 46 80 01
⊕ 11/O13

Marchand de Vin
27 r de Beaune, 7th
Ⓜ Rue du Bac
Ⓒ 01 40 15 03 26
⊕ 10/L11

Ronalba
54 r du Fbg St Denis, 10th
Ⓜ Château d'Eau
Ⓒ 01 44 83 96 30
⊕ 7/R6

Le Savoyard
39 r Popincourt, 10th
Ⓜ Saint Ambroise
Ⓒ 01 43 55 48 63
⊕ 12/W11

Vins Rares Peter Thustrup
11 r Pergolèse, 16th
Ⓜ Argentine
Ⓒ 01 45 01 46 01
⊕ 1-5/A5

Organic options

La Cave de l'Insolite
30 r de la Folie Méricourt,
11th
Ⓜ Saint Ambroise
Ⓒ 01 53 36 08 33
⊕ 8-12/W9

La Cave des Papilles
35 r Daguerre, 14th
Ⓜ Denfert Rochereau
Ⓒ 01 43 20 05 74
⊕ Off map

**L'Estaminet Arômes
et Cépages**
39 r de Bretagne, 3rd
Ⓜ Filles du Calvaire
Ⓒ 01 42 72 28 12
⊕ 11-12/T10

Flashy names and chains

Caves Bernard Magrez
43 r St-Augustin, 2nd
Ⓜ Quatre Septembre
Ⓒ 01 49 24 03 11
⊕ 7/N7

Georges Duboeuf
9 r Marbeuf, 8th
Ⓜ Alma Marceau
Ⓒ 01 47 20 71 23
⊕ 5/F7

Nicolas
31 pl de la Madeleine, 8th
Ⓜ Madeleine
Ⓒ 01 42 68 00 16
nicolasmadeleine.fr
⊕ 6/K7

Fauchon
30 pl de la Madeleine, 8th
Ⓜ Madeleine
Ⓒ 01 70 39 38 00
fauchon.fr
⊕ 6/K7

Hédiard
21 pl de la Madeleine, 8th
Ⓜ Madeleine
Ⓒ 01 43 12 88 88
hediard.fr
⊕ 6/K7

Le Repaire de Bacchus
112 r Mouffetard, 5th
Ⓜ Censier-Daubenton
Ⓒ 01 47 07 39 40
repairedebacchus.com
⊕ 15/Q17

Italian wines

06

La Bottega di Pastavino
18 r de Buci, 6th
Ⓜ Mabillon
Ⓒ 01 44 07 09 56
⊕ 11/N12

I Golosi
6 r de la Grange Batelière, 9th
Ⓒ 01 48 24 18 63
Ⓜ Grands Boulevards
⊕ 7/O7

Osteria
10 r de Sévigné, 4th
Ⓜ St Paul
Ⓒ 01 42 71 37 08
⊕ 11-12/T11

L'Enoteca
25 r Charles V, 4th
Ⓜ St Paul
Ⓒ 01 42 78 91 44
⊕ 11-12/T13

Idea Vino
88 av Parmentier, 11th
Ⓜ Parmentier
Ⓒ 01 43 57 10 34
⊕ 8/W9

Pasta et Basta
58 r du Javelot, 13th
Ⓜ Tolbiac
Ⓒ 01 44 24 54 84
⊕ Off map

The best wine bars

Autour d'un verre
21 r de Trévise, 9th
Ⓜ Grands Boulevards
Ⓒ 01 48 24 43 74
⊕ 3-5/P5

La Crèmerie
9 r des Quatre Vents, 6th
Ⓜ Mabillon
Ⓒ 01 43 54 99 30
⊕ 11/N13

Les Papilles
30 r Gay Lussac, 5th
Ⓜ Luxembourg
Ⓒ 01 43 25 20 79
⊕ 15/Q16

Le Baratin
3 r Jouye-Rouve, 20th
Ⓜ Pyrénées
Ⓒ 01 43 49 39 70
⊕ 8/Y6

Les Enfants Rouges
9 r de Beauce, 3rd
Ⓜ Filles du Calvaire
Ⓒ 08 99 78 27 91
⊕ 7/S9

Le Petit Verdot
75 r du Cherche-Midi, 6thi
Ⓜ Falguière
Ⓒ 01 42 22 38 27
le-petit-verdot.com
⊕ 14/J15

Le Café de la Nouvelle Mairie
19 r des Fossés St Jacques, 5th
⒭ Luxembourg
Ⓒ 01 44 07 04 41
⊕ 15/P15

Les Fines Gueules
2 r de la Vrillière, 1st
Ⓜ Bourse
Ⓒ 01 42 61 35 41
⊕ 7/O8

Le Rubis
10 r du Marché St Honoré, 1st
Ⓜ Tuileries
Ⓒ 01 42 61 03 34
⊕ 6/M8

Le Café du Passage
12 r de Charonne, 11th
Ⓜ Ledru-Rollin
Ⓒ 01 49 29 97 64
⊕ 12/W13

Juvénile's
47 r de Richelieu, 1st
Ⓜ Palais Royal
Ⓒ 01 42 97 46 49
⊕ 7/N9

Le Petit Verdot
75 r du Cherche-Midi, 6thi
Ⓜ Falguière
Ⓒ 01 42 22 38 27
le-petit-verdot.com
⊕ 14/J15

Le Chapeau Melon
92 r Rébeval, 19th
Ⓜ Pyrénées
Ⓒ 01 42 02 68 60
⊕ 8/Y5

La Muse Vin
101 r de Charonne, 11th
Ⓜ Charonne
Ⓒ 01 40 09 93 05
⊕ 12/Y12

Le Vin Sobre
25 r des Feuillantines, 5th
⒭ Port Royal
Ⓒ 01 43 29 00 23
⊕ 15/O17

Wine courses and tastings

Les Caprices de l'Instant
12 r Jacques Coeur, 4th
Ⓜ Bastille
Ⓒ 01 40 27 9 00
⊕ 12/U13

Grains Nobles
5 r Laplace, 5th
Ⓜ Cardinal Lemoine
Ⓒ 01 43 54 93 54
⊕ 15/P15

Legrand Filles et Fils
1 r de la Banque, 2nd
Ⓜ Bourse
Ⓒ 01 42 60 07 12
⊕ 7/O8

La Cave du Plaza Athénée
Hôtel du Plaza Athénée
25 av Montaigne, 8th
Ⓜ Alma Marceau
Ⓒ 01 53 67 66 65
⊕ 5/F8

Le Jardin des Vignes
91 r de Turenne, 3rd
Ⓜ Filles du Calvaire
Ⓒ 01 42 77 05 00
⊕ 8/U9

O Château Wine Loft
100 r de la Folie-
Méricourt, 11th
Ⓜ Goncourt
Ⓒ 01 44 73 97 80
⊕ 8/V8

Cavestève
17 r de l'Arsenal, 4th
Ⓜ Bastille
Ⓒ 01 44 59 20 20
⊕ 16/U14

Lavinia
3 bd de la Madeleine, 1st
Ⓜ Madeleine
Ⓒ 01 42 97 20 27
⊕ 6/K7

Les Vignes de Paris Bagatelle
10 rte du Champ
d'Entraînement, Bois de
Boulogne, 16th
Ⓡ Avenue Foch
Ⓒ 01 45 01 61 43
⊕ Off map

06

Late-night shopping

La Garde-Robe
41 r de l'Arbre Sec, 1st
Ⓜ Les Halles
Ⓒ 01 49 26 90 60
⊕ 11/P10

Monoprix Elysées
52 av des Champs-
Elysées, 8th
Ⓜ George V
Ⓒ 01 53 77 65 69
monoprix.fr
⊕ 5/E6

Publicis Drugstore
133 av des Champs-
Elysées, 8th
Ⓜ Charles de Gaulle-
Etoile
Ⓒ 01 44 43 79 00
publicisdrugstore.com
⊕ 5/D6

Restaurants and sommeliers

L'Alsaco
10 r Condorcet, 9th
(M) Poissonnière
(C) 01 45 26 44 31
(+) 3/P3

L'Ambroisie
9 pl des Vosges, 4th
(M) St Paul
(C) 01 42 78 51 45
(+) 12/U12

A Mi-Chemin
37 r Boulard, 14th
(M) Mouton Duvernet
(C) 01 45 39 56 45
(+) Off map

Apicius
20 r d'Artois, 8th
(M) St Phillipe du Roule
(C) 01 43 80 19 66
(+) 5-6/G6

L'Arpège
84 r de Varenne, 7th
(M) Varenne
(C) 01 47 05 09 06
(+) 10/I12

Le Bistrot du Sommelier
97 bd Haussmann, 8th
(M) St Augustin
(C) 01 42 65 24 85
(+) 2-6/I5

Le Carré des Feuillants
14 r Castiglione, 1st
(M) Tuileries
(C) 01 42 86 07 71
(+) 6/L8

Le Cinq
Hôtel George V, 31 av
George V, 8th
(M) George V
(C) 01 49 52 70 00
(+) 5/E7

Le Comptoir du Relais
7 carrefour de l'Odéon, 6th
(M) Odéon
(C) 01 43 29 12 05
(+) 11/N13

Le Crillon
10 pl Concorde, 8th
(M) Concorde
(C) 01 44 71 15 00
(+) 6/J8

Drouant
18 pl Gaillon, 2th
(M) Opéra
(C) 01 42 68 11 97
www.drouant.com
(+) 6/M7

Elysées Lenôtre
10 av Champs Elysées, 8th
(M) Champs Elycées
Clemenceau
(C) 01 42 65 85 10
(+) 6/H7

Guy Savoy
18 r Troyon, 17th
(M) Charles de Gaulle
Etoile
(C) 01 43 80 4 61
(+) 1-5/D5

Lasserre
17 av F D Roosevelt, 8th
(M) F D Roosevelt
(C) 01 43 59 53 43
(+) 6/G8

Ledoyen
Pavillon Ledoyen,
1 av Dutuit, 8th
(M) Chps Elysées Clemenceau
(C) 01 53 05 10 00
(+) 6/I8

La Maison de l'Aubrac
37 r Marbeuf, 8th
Ⓜ F D Roosevelt
📞 01 43 59 05 14
➕ 6/I7

L'Os à Moelle
3 r Vasco de Gama, 15th
Ⓜ Lourmel
📞 01 45 57 27 27
➕ 13/A17

Tan Dinh
60 r de Verneuil, 7th
Ⓜ Rue du Bac
📞 01 45 44 04 84
➕ 10/L11

La Maison Courtine
157 av du Maine, 14th
Ⓜ Mouton Duvernet
📞 01 45 43 08 04
➕ Off map

Paris Main d'Or
133 r du Fbg St Antoine, 11th
Ⓜ Ledru Rollin
📞 01 44 68 04 68
➕ 12/X13

La Tour d'Argent
15 quai de la Tournelle, 5th
Ⓜ Maubert Mutualité
📞 01 40 46 71 11
➕ 15/R14

Maître Paul
12 r Monsieur le Prince, 6th
Ⓜ Odéon
📞 01 43 54 74 59
➕ 15/O14

Le Pré Catelan
route de Suresnes, 16th
🚉 Av Henri Martin
📞 01 45 24 43 25
➕ Off map

Le Trou Gascon
40 r Taine, 12th
Ⓜ Daumesnil
📞 01 43 44 34 26
➕ Off map

06

Le Marsangy
73 av Parmentier, 11th
Ⓜ Parmentier
📞 01 47 00 94 25
➕ 8/W8

Ritz
15 pl Vendôme, 1st
Ⓜ Madeleine
📞 01 43 16 30 30
➕ 6/L8

La Truffière
4 r Blainville, 5th
Ⓜ Place Monge
📞 01 46 33 64 74
➕ 15/Q16

Le Meurice
228 r de Rivoli, 1st
Ⓜ Tuileries
📞 01 44 58 10 10
➕ 6/M9

Le Severo
8 r des Plantes, 14th
Ⓜ Mouton Duvernet
📞 01 45 40 40 91
➕ Off map

Le Villaret
13 r Ternaux, 11th
Ⓜ Parmentier
📞 01 43 57 89 76
➕ 8/W9

See page 9 to scan the directory

COOKERY SCHOOLS
AND MASTER CLASSES

L'Atelier des Chefs
10 rue de Penthièvre, 8th

Previous page: L'Atelier des Sens
40 rue Sedaine, 11th

I f you think all Parisians are born knowing how to whip up a soufflé at a moment's notice, the number of new cookery schools aimed at beginners will surprise you. It's the latest French paradox: beautiful fresh ingredients abound in the markets and food shops, yet many young people have no idea what to do with them. Blame it on their mothers, who turned their backs on what felt like kitchen slavery to join the workforce in the 1960s and 1970s, relying on convenience foods to feed their families. Even those who continued to cook often saw no need to burden their children by passing on their skills.

Today, twenty- and thirtysomethings who missed out on a culinary education are finding ways to fit cookery classes into their busy schedules. The aim is not to go back to their grandparents' way of life but to acquire skills that allow them to improvise with fresh ingredients in the time they have available. Some of the latest French cooking classes draw on spices and new techniques, while others focus on foreign cuisines, particularly Italian and Japanese. Several schools schedule classes in English or with interpreters, and it is always worth enquiring to find out if this is an option.

07

Lunchtime learning

Lack of time is the biggest obstacle for Parisians wanting to hone their cooking skills. The rapidly expanding l'**Atelier des Chefs**, which now has four branches in Paris, was the first school to come to the rescue with lunchtime cookery classes. For €15 you can join a class of up to 20 and participate in the making of a single dish. Thirty minutes later, it's time to sit down to lunch at a long table, with extras such as dessert and a glass of wine costing €2 to €3 each.

At l'**Atelier des Sens**, you might spend a lunch hour preparing zucchini flowers and lavender crème brûlée as part of a flower theme. The cooking is similarly sophisticated at l'**Académie des Cinq Sens**, where you can learn to make asparagus mousseline with sautéed morels in less than an hour. Even the **Ecole Ritz Escoffier** is in on the act with lunchtime classes for €45 on themes such as risotto and truffles.

Master classes

The unabashed use of butter and cream continues at classic cookery schools such as **Le Cordon Bleu** and the **Ecole Ritz Escoffier**, where many foreign students come to obtain diplomas in cuisine or pâtisserie. Visitors can watch a demonstration or take part in a hands-on class, the best of which are intensive workshops such as the one-week bread-baking course at Le Cordon Bleu. The **Pavillon Elysées Ecole Lenôtre** is aimed solely at amateurs but has a high standard of teaching. It too holds demonstrations and hands-on workshops. Recipes range from the retro (*boeuf en croûte, sauce Périgueux*) to the modern (monkfish *ceviche* with ginger mousse).

The ultimate in chic, though, is probably a class at the **Ecole de Cuisine Alain Ducasse** for amateurs, where you can spend half a day or a day exploring themes such as stocks, sauces and condiments, or classics from southern France. Both Lenôtre and Alain Ducasse have schools for professionals outside Paris. The **Ecole Grégoire Ferrandi** is a highly respected state school in central Paris that also holds occasional evening classes for amateurs.

07

Small and informal

Even without attending one of the big schools, you can learn from a highly trained chef. Martial Enguehard worked in top Paris restaurants including Lucas Carton and the Crillon and ran his own bistro before opening his cookery school, **Chef Martial**, in the Marais. In the mornings, you can tour the market with Martial before preparing a seasonal menu, or instead attend an evening class, cooking a classic three-course French dinner with the occasional modern twist.

Le Diet Café
9 rue Charles V, 4th

Marie Naël, former chef at the acclaimed restaurant Ecaille et Plume, also demystifies French cooking at her **Atelier Saveur et Savoir**. Her basic principles course tackles the essentials for beginners and foreigners, while in her interactive class she shows how to improvise with the freshest market produce.

Paule Caillat, founder of **Promenades Gourmandes**, has been teaching French home cooking in her Marais apartment for more than 10 years. She begins with a trip to the market, where she points out the best producers and shows you how to select line-caught fish.

Drawing on their extensive knowledge, three food writers also give cooking courses in Paris. Resplendent in her fuschia apron, Nathaly Nicolas-Ianniello, a well known French food writer, has grouped her recipes by colour at **Esprit Cuisine** to help you plan menus that look as good as they taste. The International Green menu, for, instance, features rocket pesto, monkfish with green curry, zucchini skin chips and green tea ice cream. Classes with English translations cost €100 per person. If you can't make it to Normandy to **On Rue Tatin**, the school of American cookbook author Susan Loomis, check her interesting website to see when she is teaching in the Saint-Germain cooking studio of the veteran food writer **Patricia Wells**.

07

Gourmet tours

Paris has such an overwhelming number of markets and food shops that it can be hard to know where to start. For chocoholics, **David Lebovitz's** fast-paced insider's tour of Paris chocolate shops is a must. **French Links** tours has created several food and wine tours, including one that teaches French women's secrets to staying slim. Among the many shopping themed tours offered by **Chic Shopping Paris** is the Très Tasty Tour, focusing on the finest French food and wine. The best guide to the Rungis wholesale market outside Paris is food expert and longtime Parisienne Stephanie Curtis of **Culinary Concepts**, who will take you to this awe-inspiring market before dawn. **Edible Paris**, run by Rosa Jackson, the author of this book, creates custom food itineraries for visitors based on a questionnaire that identifies their tastes

davidlebovitz.com
chicshoppingparis.com
edible-paris.com
frenchlinks.com
stecurtis@aol.com.

Fresh and healthy

If all that rich French food is too much, try a cookery workshop with **Cuisine Fraich' Attitude**, part of a government initiative to promote the consumption of fruits and vegetables. Two-hour lunchtime workshops cost €12. In the same heathy spirit Frédérique Lauwerie of **Le Diet Café** runs courses with the emphasis on balanced nutrition in a stark white kitchen in the Marais. Proving healthy can be flavourful, dishes include asparagus with truffle vinaigrette and fruit salad with Earl Grey sorbet. Or if the fresh flavours of raw fish appeal, sign up with **Manekineko de Montmartre**, where Japanese cooks teach you how to prepare nigiri, maki, gunkan maki, sushi, and sashimi for €63 (two-hour session), and traditional family Osaka cuisine for €73 (three-hour session).

07

A chef in your kitchen

If you don't manage to learn cooking in Paris, you can always hire a private chef to come to your home. **Angelo Capasa**, **Chef à la Maison**, **Chef Service** and **Les Dîners de Bérénice** will come to your home to walk you through a dinner party or, if you've really thrown in the towel, prepare the meal for you. At Chef Service you can choose from a roll call of prestigious chefs, including Laurent Veyet, Christophe Bouillant, Marie Chemorin and Alain Chalandre.

Lunchtime learning

L'Académie des Cinq Sens
25 r Royale, 8th
Ⓜ Madeleine
☎ 01 47 42 14 10
academiecinqsens.com
⊕ 6/K7

L'Atelier des Chefs
10 r de Penthièvre, 8th
Ⓜ Miromesnil
☎ 01 53 30 05 82
atelierdeschefs.com
⊕ 6/I6

L'Atelier des Sens
40 r Sedaine, 11th
Ⓜ Voltaire
☎ 01 40 21 08 50
atelier-des-sens.com
⊕ 12/W11

Master classes

Le Cordon Bleu
8 r L Delhomme, 15th
Ⓜ Vaugirard
☎ 01 53 68 22 50
cordonbleu.edu
⊕ 13/E17

Ecole des Gourmets
111 av Daumesnil, 12th
Ⓜ Montgallet
☎ 01 43 40 20 20
ecoledesgourmets.fr
⊕ 16/Z17

Ecole Ritz Escoffier
38 r Cambon, 1st
Ⓜ Madeleine
☎ 01 43 16 30 50
ritzparis.com
⊕ 6/K8

L'Ecole de Cuisine d'Alain Ducasse
55 bd Malesherbes, 8th
Ⓜ St-Augustin
☎ 01 44 90 91 00
atelier-gastronomique.com
⊕ 6/J6

L'Ecole Grégoire Ferrandi
28 r de l'Abbé Grégoire, 6th
Ⓜ Saint-Placide
☎ 01 49 54 28 00
egf.ccip.fr/accueil.asp
⊕ 14/K15

Pavillon Elysées Ecole Lenôtre
10 av des Champs Elysées, 8th
Ⓜ Franklin D. Roosevelt
☎ 01 42 65 97 60
lenotre.fr
⊕ 6/H7

Fresh and healthy

Cuisine Fraich'Attitude
60 r du Fbg Poissonnière, 9th
Ⓜ Bonne Nouvelle
☎ 01 49 49 15 15
cuisinefraichattitude.com
⊕ 7/Q6

Le Diet Café
9 r Charles V, 4th
Ⓜ Sully Morland
☎ 01 42 74 07 85
e-dietcafe.com
⊕ 11-12/T13

Manekineko de Montmartre
1bis r Garreau, 18th
Ⓜ Abbesses
☎ 01 42 64 52 78
⊕ 3/N1

Promenades Gourmandes
187 rue du Temple, 3rd

Small and informal

**Astuces et tours
de main**
29 r Censier, 5th
Ⓜ Censier-Daubenton
Ⓣ 01 45 87 11 37
astucesettousdemains.com
⊕ 15/A17

Chef Martial
r des Tournelles, 3th
Ⓜ Richard Lenoir
Ⓣ 01 44 54 02 18
chefmartial.com
⊕ 12/U11

On Rue Tatin
Louviers, Normandie
onruetatin.com
⊕ Off map

L'Atelier de Fred
Pass de l'Ancre,
223 r St-Martin, 3rd
Ⓜ Arts et Métiers
Ⓣ 01 40 29 46 04
latelierdefred.com
⊕ 7/R9

Esprit Cuisine
68 r Amelot, 11th
Ⓜ St-Sébastien-Froissart
Ⓣ 01 43 57 12 31
espritcuisine.com
⊕ 12/V12

Patricia Wells
Atelier: r Jacob, 6th
Ⓜ St-Germain-des-Prés
patriciawells.com
⊕ 10/M12

Atelier Saveur et Savoir
25 bis r Duvivier, 7th
Ⓜ Ecole Militaire
Ⓣ 01 47 53 84 67
atelier-saveur-savoir.fr
⊕ 9-10/G11

Olivier Berté
7 r Paul Lelong, 2nd
Ⓜ Bourse
Ⓣ 01 40 26 14 00
coursdecuisineparis.com
⊕ 7/O8

Promenades Gourmandes
187 r du Temple, 3rd
Ⓜ République
Ⓣ 01 48 04 56 84
promenadesgourmandes.com
⊕ 7/S9

A chef in your kitchen

Angelo Capasa
68 r Villiers de l'Isle
Adam, 20th
Ⓜ Pelleport
Ⓒ 06 61 54 86 37
⊕ Off map

Chef à Domicile
Ⓒ 01 48 80 17 43
chefadomicile.fr

Chef à la Maison
37 r Popincourt, 11th
Ⓜ Voltaire
Ⓒ 01 43 38 45 92
chefalamaison.fr
⊕ 12/X11

Chef Service
36 r Etienne Marcel, 2nd
Ⓜ Etienne Marcel
Ⓒ 0872 349721
chef-service.com
⊕ 7/P9

Les Dîners de Bérénice
Ⓒ 01 46 38 86 42
lesdinersdeberenice.fr

Marc Girard
Ⓒ 06 22 47 33 18
marc-girard.com

07

MaxMijote
40 r Madeleine Michelis
Neuilly sur Seine
Ⓜ Pont de Neuilly
Ⓒ 06 60 42 02 09
⊕ Off map

See page 9
to scan the
directory

CITY SECRETS
FROM FOODIES

E. Dehillerin
51 rue Jean-Jacques Rousseau, 1st

Previous page: Maille
6 Place de la Madeleine, 8th

It's not unusual in Paris to come across a chef shopping at an open-air food market, sniffing the melons for that heady summer aroma or gently prodding an avocado to test for ripeness. With so many markets and food shops to choose from, it makes sense for chefs to take a hands-on approach rather than leave all the shopping to someone else. The bravest of them get up in the wee hours to drive to the southern suburb of Rungis, where the biggest wholesale market in Europe takes place every day except Sunday. As this trip requires enormous stamina given the typical chef's late working hours, most use a combination of trusted suppliers and perhaps a local market for produce. Although the wholesale market moved out of Les Halles, in the centre of Paris, in the late 1960s, a handful of wholesale butchers, fishmongers and luxury food shops have survived here alongside professional kitchenware shops.

08

Kitchenware shops

Ask any chef where he buys his pots and pans and he will most likely name **E. Dehillerin**. Founded in 1820, this concrete-floored warehouse doesn't seem to have changed much since. Staff greet you at the door, and the narrow aisles are often clogged with French and foreign chefs examining the lidded *pain de mie* tins, carbon steel knives, copper pots and more modern implements such as silicone *madeleine* moulds and microplane graters.

Chef William Ledeuil, who is known for his Asian-inspired cooking at **Ze Kitchen Galerie**, appreciates the kitchenware shop **La Bovida** and the baking specialist **Mora**, both around the corner from Dehillerin. Cookery teacher Paule Caillat of Promenades Gourmandes buys her prized Le Creuset pots at Dehillerin, but has a soft spot for **Kitchen Bazaar**, "for the modern brands like Good Grips that you can't find at Dehillerin." Pastry chef and renowned food blogger David Lebovitz likes the **BHV** department store for its broad selection and reasonable prices.

Markets and supermarkets

The chefs' most beloved market is **Président Wilson**, mainly because of market gardener Joël Thiébault's extraordinary selection of vegetables. You might see Ledeuil here, or Flora Mikula of the nearby contemporary restaurant **Les Saveurs de Flora**. Thiébault also delivers to restaurants such as **Pétrelle** and **Mon Vieil Ami**. "I could have my vegetables delivered but I like to go and have a look, because seeing the produce gives me ideas," says Ledeuil. Daniel Rose of the popular new bistro **Spring** finds his inspiration at the **Place des Fêtes** market in the 19th, and Ina Garten, aka the Barefoot Contessa of US television fame, can sometimes be seen at the **Raspail Market** near her Paris apartment, on the Rive Gauche side of Paris.

Ledeuil, who likes to shop at Asian supermarkets for ingredients such as galangal, Thai basil, lemongrass and hard-to-find varieties of mango, prefers smaller supermarkets in the 13th, such as **Big Store** and **Exo Store**, to the gigantic **Tang Frères**, which can be overwhelming. When buying in quantity, Lebovitz goes to the **Place d'Aligre** market for eggs, cream and butter at good prices; at the same market he gets his nuts and dried fruit from Sabah, whose high turnover means that the products are always fresh. For fresh fruit and vegetables he favours **Bastille** market on boulevard Richard Lenoir. "I need to touch everything before I buy so I go to people who let me touch," says the chef.

08

Specialist shops

Specialist shops are a must for Paris chefs, who insist on the best. For top-quality French meat the name that they quote most often is **Boucherie Hugo Desnoyer** in quartier Daguerre, whose client list includes l'Ambroisie, Pierre Gagnaire, Astrance, Hiramatsu and the Ritz, and wine bars Le Verre Volé and Le Severo.

Quatrehomme
62 rue de Sèvres, 7th

Paule Caillat buys meat for her classes at the **Boucherie du Marais** on rue de Bretagne, near the Enfants Rouges market, and charcuterie from **Joël Meurdesoif**, who produces melt-in-the-mouth pâtés for many Paris wine bars. Ledeuil has a wholesale supplier for fish, but shops at **La Poissonnerie du Dôme** or a branch of **Daguerre Marée** if he is cooking at home. **Marie-Anne Cantin**, **Quatrehomme**, **Fromages Dubois** and **Fromagerie Alléosse** supply astonishing cheeses to many of the best restaurants in Paris, while **Barthélemy** caters to a celebrity clientele from its tiny shop in Saint-Germain-des-Prés.

When it comes to cookware, Caillat can't imagine life without quirky pastry supply shop **G. Detou**, the only place she knows in Paris where you can buy giant bags of Valrhona chocolate of various origins. The secret weapon in the cooking of Basque chef Christian Etchebest at his restaurant **Le Troquet** is Banyuls vinegar, from near the Spanish border on France's Mediterranean coast, which he can conveniently buy around the corner at **Beau et Bon**. Truffles are a must in winter, and many professionals count on **Le Comptoir Corrézien** for fair prices on superb *tuber melanosporum* black truffles. A sign of changing times is that chefs often name their suppliers on their menus, giving due credit to those who provide stunning raw materials.

08

Le Bistrot Paul Bert
18 rue Paul Bert, 11th

Insider favourites

Where do food professionals go when they want to treat themselves? David Lebovitz, author of *The Perfect Scoop*, believes that **Berthillon** is still the best place in town for ice cream, even if it's hardly undiscovered. The newer **Pozzetto**, founded in Turin, is his favourite place for Italian-style *gelato*, and he likes the ice cream parlour **Raimo** for the 1950s atmosphere and freshly made ices. Paule Caillat is a fan of the new pâtisserie **Des Gâteaux et du Pain** in the quartier Falguière in the 14th, and **Arnaud Delmontel** in south Pigalle. François Simon (francoissimon.typepad.fr), the food critic at *Le Figaro* who is both respected and feared for his strong opinions, likes the vintage bistro setting and friendly atmosphere of **Le Bistrot Paul Bert** for a night out with a group of friends. A place he warmly recommends is the café **Le Petit Vendôme**, on the way from the Olympia music hall to the Tuileries garden, for its perfect sandwiches made with baguettes from Boulangerie Julien. Another restaurant well liked by the critic Gilles Pudlowski is **Entre les Vignes**. Near Gare de Lyon, it serves traditional French cuisine to gourmet travellers on their way to the South of France or Italy before they board the train.

08

Kitchenware shops

BHV
52 r de Rivoli, 4th
Ⓜ Hôtel de Ville
Ⓒ 01 42 74 90 00
bhv.fr
⊕ 11/S12

La Bovida
36 r Montmartre, 1st
Ⓜ Etienne Marcel
Ⓒ 01 42 36 09 99
⊕ 7/P8

E. Dehillerin
51, r J-J Rousseau, 1st
Ⓜ Palais Royal
Ⓒ 01 42 36 53 13
e-dehillerin.fr
⊕ 7/O9

Kitchen Bazaar
50 r Croix-des-Petits-Champs, 1st
Ⓜ Pyramides
Ⓒ 01 40 15 03 11
kitchenbazaar.fr
⊕ 7/O9

Mora
13 r de Montmartre, 1st
Ⓜ Etienne Marcel
Ⓒ 01 45 08 19 24
mora.fr
⊕ 7/P8

Simon
48 r de Montmartre, 2nd
Ⓜ Etienne Marcel
Ⓒ 01 42 33 71 65
simon-a.com
⊕ 7/P8

Markets and supermarkets

Aligre market
Tue-Sun 8am-1pm
r d'Aligre
Ⓜ Ledru-Rollin
marchedaligre.free.fr
⊕ 16/X14

Bastille market
Thur and Sun 8am-1.30pm
Bd Richard Lenoir, 11th
Ⓜ Bastille
⊕ 12/V11

Big Store
81 av d'Ivry, 13th
Ⓜ Porte d'Ivry
Ⓒ 01 44 24 28 88
⊕ Off map

Exo Store
52 av de Choisy, 13th.
Ⓜ Tolbiac
Ⓒ 01 44 24 99 88
⊕ Off map

Inno Montparnasse
31 r du Départ, 14th
Ⓜ Montparnasse
Ⓒ 01 43 20 69 30
⊕ 14/K16

Place des Fêtes market
Tue, Fri and Sun 8am-1.30pm
Pl des Fêtes,19th
Ⓜ Place des Fêtes
⊕ Off map

Président Wilson market
Wed and Sat 8am-1.30pm
Av du Président Wilson, 16th
Ⓜ Iéna
⊕ 14/L15

Raspail market
*Tue, Fri, Sun 8am-1.30pm
(organic on Sun)*
bd Raspail
Ⓜ Rennes
⊕ 14/L15

Rungis wholesale market
1 r de la Tour
94152 Rungis
Ⓒ 01 41 80 80 00
visiterungis.com
⊕ Off map

Specialist shops

Barthélemy
51 r de Grenelle, 7th
Ⓜ Rue du Bac
Ⓒ 01 45 48 56 75
⊕ 10/K12

Le Comptoir Corrézien
8 r des Volontaires, 15th
Ⓜ Sèvres Lecourbe
Ⓒ 01 47 83 52 97
⊕ 13-14/G16

Joël Meurdesoif
8 r Albert Bayet, 13th
Ⓜ Place d'Italie
Ⓒ 01 42 16 81 83
⊕ Off map

Beau et Bon
81 r Lecourbe, 15th
Ⓜ Sèvres Lecourbe
Ⓒ 01 43 06 06 53
beauetbon.free.fr
⊕ 13/F16

Daguerre Marée
9 r Daguerre, 14th
Ⓜ Denfert Rochereau
Ⓒ 01 43 22 13 52
⊕ Off map

Marie-Anne Cantin
12 r du Champ de Mars, 7th
Ⓜ Ecole Militaire.
Ⓒ 01 45 50 43 94
cantin.fr
⊕ 9/F12

La Bottega di Piacenza
53 rue des Abbesses, 18th
Ⓜ Abbesses
Ⓒ 01 44 92 90 99
⊕ 3/N1

Fromagerie Alléosse
13 r Poncelet, 17th
Ⓜ Ternes
Ⓒ 01 46 22 50 45.
fromage-allcosse.com/
⊕ 1/E3

La Poissonnerie du Dôme
4 r Delambre, 14th
Ⓜ Vavin
Ⓒ 01 43 35 23 95
⊕ 14/L17

Boucherie Hugo Desnoyer
25 r Mouton-Duvernet, 14th
Ⓜ Mouton-Duvernet
Ⓒ 01 45 40 76 67
regalez-vous.com
⊕ Off map

Fromages Dubois
2 r de Lourmel, 15th
Ⓜ Lourmel
Ⓒ 01 45 78 70 58
⊕ 13/A17

Pozzetto
39 r du Roi de Sicile , 4th
Ⓜ Saint-Paul
Ⓒ 01 42 77 08 44
pozzetto.biz
⊕ 11/S12

08

Boucherie du Marais
17 r de Bretagne, 3rd
Ⓜ Filles du Calvaire
Ⓒ 01 42 77 21 94
⊕ 7-8/T9

G. Detou
58 r Tiquetonne, 2nd
Ⓜ Etienne Marcel
Ⓒ 01 42 36 54 67
⊕ 7/Q9

Qualitalia
38 r Broca, 5th
Ⓜ Les Gobelins
Ⓒ 01 47 07 11 44
qualitalia.fr
⊕ 15/Q17

Marché d'Aligre
rue d'Aligre

Insider favourites

Entre les Vignes
27ter bd Diderot, 12th
Ⓜ Poissonnière
Ⓒ 01 43 43 62 84
⊕ 16/V15

Le Bistrot Paul Bert
18 r Paul Bert, 11th
Ⓜ Faidherbe-Chaligny
Ⓒ 01 43 72 24 01
⊕ 12/Y13

Le Petit Vendôme
8 r des Capucines, 2nd
Ⓜ Opéra
Ⓒ 01 42 61 05 88
⊕ 6/L7

Arnaud Delmontel
39 r des Martyrs, 9th
Ⓜ Saint-Georges
Ⓒ 01 48 78 29 33
arnaud-delmontel.com
⊕ 3/O4

Des Gâteaux et du Pain
63 bd Pasteur, 15th
Ⓜ Pasteur
Ⓒ 01 45 38 94 16
⊕ 14/H16

Pozzetto
39 r du Roi de Sicile, 4th
Ⓜ Saint-Paul
Ⓒ 01 42 77 08 44
pozzetto.biz
⊕ 11/S12

Berthillon
31 r St-Louis-en-l'Ile, 4th
Ⓜ Sully-Morland
Ⓒ 01 43 54 31 61
berthillon.fr
⊕ 11/S13

Isami
4 quai d'Orléans, 4th
Ⓜ Pont-Marie
Ⓒ 01 40 46 06 97
⊕ 11/R13

Raimo Glacier
59-61 bd de Reuilly
Ⓜ Daumesnil
Ⓒ 01 43 43 70 17
raimoglaciers.com
⊕ Off map

Where the chefs rule

Mon Vieil Ami
Fréderic Crochet
69 r Saint-Louis en l'Ile, 4th
Ⓜ Pont Marie
Ⓒ 01 40 46 01 35
⊕ 11/S13

Les Saveurs de Flora
Flora Mikula
36 av George V, 8th
Ⓜ George V
Ⓒ 01 40 70 10 49
lessaveursdeflora.com/
⊕ 5/E7

Le Troquet
Christian Etchebest
21 r Fr Bonvin, 15th
Ⓜ Sèvres-Lecourbe
Ⓒ 01 45 66 89 00
⊕ 13-14/G16

08

Pétrelle
Jean-Luc André
34 r de Pétrelle, 9th
Ⓜ Anvers
Ⓒ 01 42 82 11 02
⊕ 3/Q3

Spring
Daniel Rose
28 r de la Tour
d'Auvergne, 9th
Ⓜ Anvers
Ⓒ 01 45 96 05 72
springparis.blogspot.com/
⊕ 3/O3

Ze Kitchen Galerie
William Ledeuil
4 r des Gds Augustins, 6th
ⓇⒺⓇ Saint-Michel
Ⓒ 01 44 32 00 32
zekitchengalerie.fr
⊕ 11/O12

See page 9
to scan the
directory

 BERNARDAUD

09

THE ART OF
FINE DINING

Gargantua
1 rue Charlemagne, 4th

Previous page: Bernardaud
11 rue Royale, 8th

The French reputation for gastronomy doesn't rest on food alone. Every element contributes to the pleasure of a good meal, from the choice of plates and silverware to the shape of the wine glasses and colour of the table cloth. If most bistros keep it simple with white plates, basic wine glasses and, sometimes, no tablecloths at all, haute cuisine restaurants pull out all the stops with Limoges porcelain, Christofle silverware and crystal glasses.

At home, we show our sense of style through tableware and linens. White minimalism, brightly hued glass and Scandinavian or Asian-influenced designs are a few modern looks, but classic French patterns from the 18th and 19th centuries have eternal appeal. There can be few better places in the world to shop for tableware than Paris.

Department store homeware

The most efficient way to see a range of styles is to visit one of the major department stores. Across from the Galeries Lafayette on boulevard Haussmann is **Lafayette Maison**, a multilevel store dedicated to the

09

home. In the basement you will find small kitchen appliances and equipment. and a glassed-in branch of the cooking school l'Atelier des Chefs, while tableware is spread out over the next two floors. Just as impressive is the redesigned Arts de la Maison space in the **Bon Marché**, where you'll find classic names such as Lalique, Baccarat and Cristal de Sèvres, alongside lines such as Spanish chef Ferran Adrià's El Bulli Collection of table linen and trendy chefs' clothes. On the second floor of **Printemps de la Maison** there are mini-boutiques dedicated to luxury products, such as tea from Mariage Frères, wine from Les Caves Taillevent and chocolate from Jean-Paul Hévin, adding another dimension to shopping for tableware. **BHV**'s tableware section has a particularly practical layout.

Porcelain and ceramics

Department stores have only a limited selection from each brand, so it's often worthwhile to seek out individual boutiques. A legendary name in porcelain is **Bernardaud**, whose designs range from the sober to the sumptuous. It has introduced several all-white lines with a minimalist modern aesthetic called 'White is magnifique'. Just as chic is **Haviland**, a Limoges company dating from 1842 that over the decades has enlisted the talents of artists such as Dufy, Cocteau and Dali. **Gien**, founded in France in 1821 by Englishman Thomas Hall, remains resolutely traditional in its faience, though a line of white dishes by designer Patrick Jouin adds a touch of modernity. The **Manufacture Nationale de Sèvres** supplied fine porcelain to the kings of France from 1740 and now replaces government tableware. A wealth of historic designs can be found in its shop near the Palais Royal.

Established more recently, but drawing on French and Italian designs from the 17th and 18th centuries, is **Astier de Villatte**, whose main boutique is on rue Saint-Honoré. The white-glazed earthenware there is irresistible to anyone who loves pottery, but tires of coloured dishes. Just as unusual is **Artichaut**, whose Luberon-based founders borrow from their Russian, Hungarian and Bavarian roots to create baroque designs, such as a sugar bowl with a dome-like lid.

Emery & Cie, famous for its hand-made Moroccan *zellige* tiles, now sells earthenware dishes in beautiful hues, sometimes with dragon or flower motifs. The young company **Gargantua** produces porcelain and sandstone dishes for clients such as Habitat; pet-loving Parisians drop into the Marais showroom (open in the afternoons only) for its stylish dog and cat food bowls. A number of shops in Paris sell basic white porcelain dishes in all shapes and sizes at very reasonable prices; one of the best is **Casa Pascal** in Saint-Germain-des-Prés.

09

Artichaut
22 rue de l'Echaudé, 6th

Glass and crystal

Glasses have always played an important role on the French table and designers are growing more imaginative, using new shapes for wine and bright colours for water. Unabashedly elitist is **Baccarat**, whose slogan is "beauty is not reasonable". Its oenology line is designed for serious wine drinkers, with a different classic shape for each style of wine. The large Bordeaux wine glasses cost €150 each. Baccarat even produces crystal beer glasses, one for lagers and the other for ales. Also aiming for a timeless look is **Lalique**, whose glasses blend into classic or contemporary settings.

More accessibly priced, but still very elegant, is **Mikasa**'s Œnologie line, available in department stores. It comes in two styles: one classically curved, the other angular to draw out the wine's aromas. If you're uncertain which glass or carafe to choose, visit **l'Or du Vin**, which has a full range of glasses and every accessory you could imagine. More whimsical is **Clotilde Buschini**, who sells wine glasses with S-shaped stems, and curved water and whisky glasses in bright colours. Classic Riedel, Spiegelau and Mikasa wine glasses can be found at **Lavinia,** and **l'Esprit et le Vin,** in the 17th, also has good tasting glasses. At **Quartz**, in the 6th, you'll find glasses and carafes created by artists.

09

Etiquette classes

With a little practice anyone can become a gracious Parisian host. At least, that's the principle of **La Belle Ecole**, which offers classes in culinary skills, flower-arranging, the decorative arts and etiquette. Its "l'Art de la Table" course reveals the secrets to setting a contemporary or classic table, with expert touches to reflect the mood of the occasion, while "La French Etiquette" uses role playing to teach how to use Gallic charm instead of blowing a fuse in the office or at a restaurant. Most intriguing of all is the crash course in gallantry, "for men who have understood that courtesy is the number one weapon in the art of seduction." The next Frenchman who holds the door for you might well be a graduate.

La Belle Ecole,
7 rue Scheffer, 16th

Silverware and cutlery

Well-heeled Parisians adore **Christofle**'s silverware lines by Andrée Putman and pâtissier Pierre Hermé. Hermé's dessert forks inlaid with pastel colours are perfect for nibbling at his sculpted gâteaux. Equally appealing to cutlery aficionados is **Puiforcat**, long famed for its three-pronged fork. **Geneviève Lethu** has multicoloured tasting spoons that are hard to resist. Finally, no French household would be complete without at least one folding **Forge de Laguiole** knife. Several shops around Paris carry the brand, whose trademark is a bee on the handle. One of the last remaining silversmiths in Paris is **François Cadoret**, whose workshop in the Marais is open to the public.

Table linen

You'll find the biggest selection of traditional linen at **Le Jacquard Français**, which is divided into spaces devoted to the table, beauty and babies. Colours range from subtle to bright, with many shades of green, plum and pink. To make more of a statement, choose from vivid, striped Basque fabrics at **Jean Vier**. For Provençal tablecloths visit **La Tuile à Loup**, which also sells pottery from the South of France. **Muriel Grateau** sells everything you need to set an elegant French table: earth-toned linens, silverware and candles. The caviar and champagne are up to you.

09

Fine dining boutiques

7 Famille
114 r St-Dominique, 7th
Ⓜ Ecole Militaire
Ⓒ 01 45 51 73 25
⊕ 9/F11

Art & Sud Déco
52 pl du Marché Saint-
Honoré, 1st
Ⓜ Opéra
Ⓒ 01 42 86 95 76
artetsud.com
⊕ 6/M8

Bô
8 r Saint Merri , 4th
Ⓜ Hôtel de Ville
Ⓒ 01 42 72 84 64
⊕ 11/R10

Bohêmia
5 r du Pas-de-la-Mule, 4th
Ⓜ Chemin Vert
Ⓒ 01 42 74 22 92
⊕ 12/U12

La Chaise Longue
20 r des Francs-Bourgeois,
3rd
Ⓜ Rambuteau
Ⓒ 01 48 04 36 37
lachaiselongue.com
⊕ 11-12/T11

Déjeuner sur l'herbe
15 r Vergniaud, 92300
Levallois Perret
Ⓜ Louise Michel
Ⓒ 01 47 57 53 30
dejeunersurlherbe.fr
⊕ Off map

Dîners En Ville
27 r de Varenne, 7th
Ⓜ Rue du Bac
Ⓒ 01 42 22 78 33
⊕ 10/K12

D.O.T.
47 r de Saintonge, 3rd
Ⓜ Filles du Calvaire
Ⓒ 01 40 29 90 34
dot-france.com
⊕ 7-8/T9

Galerie Van Der Straeten
Ⓜ r Ferdinand Duval, 4th
◯ Saint Paul
Ⓒ 01 42 78 99 99
⊕ 11/S12

Home Autour du Monde
8 r des Francs-Bourgeois, 3rd
Ⓜ Rambuteau
Ⓒ 01 42 77 06 08
⊕ 11-12/T11

Kimonoya
11 r du Pt L-Philippe, 4th
Ⓜ Pont Marie
Ⓒ 01 48 87 30 24
kimonoya.fr
⊕ 11/R12

Laure Japy
34 r du Bac, 7th
Ⓜ Rue du Bac
Ⓒ 01 41 44 73 50
⊕ 10/K1

Maison de Famille
Pl de la Madeleine, 8th
Ⓜ Madeleine
Ⓒ 01 53 45 82 00
⊕ 6/K7

Siècle
24 r du Bac, 7th
Ⓜ Rue du Bac
Ⓒ 01 47 03 48 03
siecle-paris.com
⊕ 10/K12

Xanadou
10 r Saint Sulpice, 6th
Ⓜ Odéon
Ⓒ 01 43 26 73 43
⊕ 11/N13

Porcelain and ceramics

Artichaut
22 r de l'Echaudé, 6th
Ⓜ Mabillon
Ⓒ 01 40 46 84 70
artichaut.com
🜨 11/N12

Astier de Villatte
173 r Saint Honoré, 1st
Ⓜ Palais Royal
Ⓒ 01 42 60 74 13
🜨 6/M9

L'Atelier de Porcelaine
S. Mazy
3/ r de Verneuil, 7th
Ⓜ Rue du Bac
Ⓒ 01 47 24 40 15
🜨 10/L11

Atelier Le Tallec
95 av Daumesnil, 12th
Ⓜ Reuilly-Diderot
Ⓒ 01 43 40 61 55
atelierletallec.com
🜨 16/Y16

Bernardaud
11 r Royale, 8th
Ⓜ Concorde
Ⓒ 01 47 42 82 66
bernardaud.fr
🜨 6/K7

Casa Pascal
15 r d'Assas, 6th
Ⓜ Rennes
Ⓒ 01 42 22 96 78
🜨 10-14/L14

Deshoulières
14 av de l'Opéra, 1st
Ⓜ Opéra
Ⓒ 01 42 46 43 74
🜨 6/M7

Emery & Cie
18 passage de la Main
d'Or, 11th
Ⓜ Bastille
Ⓒ 01 44 87 02 22
emeryetcie.com
🜨 12/X13

Gargantua
1 r de Charlemagne, 4th
Ⓜ Saint-Paul
gargunatua.ch
🜨 11-12/T12

Gien
18 r de l'Arcade, 8th
Ⓜ Madeleine
Ⓒ 01 42 66 52 32
gien.com
🜨 6/K6

Haviland
25 r Royale, 8th
Ⓜ Madeleine
Ⓒ 01 42 66 36 36
🜨 6/K7

Manufacture Nationale
de Sèvres
4 pl André Malraux, 1st
Ⓜ Palais Royal
Ⓒ 01 47 03 40 20
amisdesevres.com
🜨 6/M9

Porcelaines M.P. Samic
45 av du Gl Leclerc, 14th
Ⓜ Alésia
Ⓒ 01 40 47 59 21
🜨 Off map

Porcelaine de Sologne
32 r de Paradis, 10th
Ⓜ Poissonnière
Ⓒ 01 42 46 43 74
🜨 3-7/Q5

Raynaud
Galerie Royale,
9 r Royale, 9th
Ⓜ Madeleine
Ⓒ 01 40 17 01 00
🜨 6/K7

09

Table linen

Frette
49 r du Fbg St Honoré, 8th
Ⓜ Concorde
Ⓣ 01 42 66 47 70
frette.com
✛ 6/J7

Le Jacquard Français
12 r Chevalier St-George,
1st
Ⓜ Concorde
Ⓣ 01 42 97 40 49
le-jacquard-français.fr
✛ 6/K7

Jean Vier
66 r de Vaugirard, 6th
Ⓜ Rennes
Ⓣ 01 45 44 26 74
jeanvierparis.fr
✛ 14/K15

Muriel Grateau
37 r de Beaune, 7th
Ⓜ Rue du Bac
Ⓣ 01 40 20 42 82
✛ 10/L11

Porthault
50 av Montaigne, 8th
Ⓜ Alma Marceau
Ⓣ 01 47 20 75 25
dporthault.fr
✛ 5/F8

La Tuile à Loup
35 r Daubenton, 5th
Ⓜ Censier-Daubenton
Ⓣ 01 47 07 28 90
latuilealoup.com
✛ 15/R17

Tea services

Maison de la Théière
17 r de l'Odéon, 6th
Ⓜ Odéon
Ⓣ 01 46 33 98 96
✛ 11/N13

Le Thé Bleu
15 r Linné, 5th
Ⓜ Place Monge
Ⓣ 01 43 36 43 36
✛ 15/R16

Zenzoo Thesaurus
2 r Chabanais, 2nd
Ⓜ Pyramides
Ⓣ 01 42 96 17 32
zen-zoo.com
✛ 7/N8

Etiquette classes

La Belle Ecole
7 r Scheffer, 16th
Ⓜ Trocadéro
Ⓣ 01 47 04 50 20
✛ 9/B10

Marie Blanche de Broglie
18 av de la Motte-Picquet,
7th
Ⓜ Ecole Militaire
Ⓣ 01 45 51 36 34
cuisinemb.com
✛ 9-10/G12

Vanessa Braco
Prétexte Gourmand
46 r des Dames, 17th
Ⓜ Place de Clichy
Ⓣ 01 55 06 09 69
pretextegourmand.com
✛ 11/O10

Glass and crystal

Baccarat
11 pl de la Madeleine, 8th
Ⓜ Madeleine
ⓒ 01 42 65 36 26
baccarat.fr
✛ 6/K7

Daum
4 r de la Paix, 2nd
ⓒ 01 42 61 25 25
Ⓜ Opéra
daum.fr
✛ 6/M7

Lavinia
3 bd de la Madeleine, 1st
Ⓜ Madeleine
ⓒ 01 42 97 20 20
lavinia.fr
✛ 6/K7

Clotilde Duschini
83 r du Cherche-Midi, 6th
Ⓜ Vaneau
ⓒ 01 45 44 30 11
✛ 14/K14

Eclat de Verres
12 r Hippolyte Lebas, 9th
Ⓜ Notre-Dame de
Lorette
ⓒ 01 48 78 05 97
vezec.com
✛ 3/O4

L'Or du Vin
81 av Ternes, 17th
Ⓜ Porte Maillot
ⓒ 01 45 72 01 90
✛ 1/B3

Cristal d'Arques
6 pl des Etats-Unis, 16th
Ⓜ Kléber
ⓒ 01 47 23 31 34
cristaldarquesparis.com
✛ 5/D7

L'Esprit et le Vin
81 av des Ternes, 17th
Ⓜ Ternes
ⓒ 01 45 74 80 99
espritetlevin.fr
✛ 1/D4

Quartz
12 r des Quatre Vents, 6th
Ⓜ Odéon
ⓒ 01 43 54 03 00
quartz-verreries.com
✛ 11/N13

Cristal Saint-Louis
13 r Royale, 8th
Ⓜ Madeleine
ⓒ 01 40 17 01 74
✛ 6/K7

Lalique
11 r Royale, 8th
Ⓜ Madeleine
ⓒ 01 53 05 12 12
✛ 6/K7

Verre Passion
16 r des Taillandiers,
11th
Ⓜ Bastille
ⓒ 01 47 00 05 93
verrepassion.com
✛ 12/W12

09

Forge de Laguiole
29, rue Boissy-d'Anglas, 8th

Silverware and cutlery

A La Mine d'Argent
108 r du Bac, 7th
Ⓒ 01 45 48 70 68
minedargent.com
⊕ 10/K13

François Cadoret
172 r de Charonne, 11th
Ⓜ Alexandre Dumas
Ⓒ 01 43 71 25 04
orfevreriedumarais.com
⊕ 12/Z12

Puiforcat
2, av Matignon, 8th
Ⓜ Franklin-Roosevelt
Ⓒ 01 45 63 10 10
⊕ 6/H7

Christofle
9 r Royale, 8th
Ⓜ Madeleine
Ⓒ 01 55 27 99 00
christofle.com
⊕ 6/K7

Geneviève Lethu
95 r de Rennes, 6th
Ⓜ Rennes
Ⓒ 01 45 44 40 35
genevievelethu.fr
⊕ 14/L14

Sabre
4 r des Quatre Vents, 6th
Ⓜ Odéon
Ⓒ 44 07 37 64
sabre.fr
⊕ 11/N13

Forge de Laguiole
29, r Boissy d'Anglas, 8th
Ⓜ Madeleine
Ⓒ 01 40 06 09 75
forge-de-laguiole.com
⊕ 6/J7

Pierre Meurgey
20 bd F du Calvaire, 11th
Ⓜ Filles du Calvaire
Ⓒ 01 48 05 82 65
meurgey.com
⊕ 12/U10

Guy Degrenne
26 r Boissy d'Anglas, 8th
Ⓜ Madeleine
Ⓒ 01 40 06 01 93
boutique.royale@
guydegrenne.fr
⊕ 6/K7

In department stores

BHV
14 r du Temple, 4th
Ⓜ Hôtel de Ville
Ⓒ 01 42 74 90 00
⊕ 11/R10

Lafayette Maison
35 bd Haussmann, 9th
Ⓜ Havre Caumartin
Ⓒ 01 40 23 53 52
⊕ 2-6/K5

Printemps
64 bd Haussmann, 9th
Ⓜ Havre Caumartin
Ⓒ 01 42 82 50 00
⊕ 2-6/K5

09

Le Bon Marché
24 r de Sèvres, 7th
Ⓜ Sèvres Babylone
Ⓒ 01 44 39 80 00
lebonmarche.fr
⊕ 10-14/K13-14

See page 9
to scan the
directory

FOODIE EVENTS
AND ONLINE HITS

Goûts de France
goutsdefrance.com

Previous page: Le Haut du Panier
lehautdupanier.com

Whether you live in Paris or visit occasionally, you can take advantage of special events, websites and blogs to deepen your knowledge of French food and wine. All year round, food exhibitions aimed at the general public provide insight into the products of various French regions or a single food item such as chocolate or cheese. From abroad, you can satisfy the most specific cravings for French food and wine by mail order, while those who live in Paris are increasingly making use of delivery services to lighten the shopping load. Guide books, websites and food blogs are invaluable in keeping up with the fast-changing Paris restaurant scene, and many websites have forums for exchanging comments and advice.

Food and wine events

Food and wine exhibitions, usually held at the Porte de Versailles or Espace Champerret, are a great way to learn more about the regions of France through their products and cuisine. The biggest and probably the most popular event is the **Salon de l'Agriculture** that takes place every year in early March at Porte de Versailles. Urban dwellers come not only to admire

10

the prize-winning farm animals on display, but also to browse at hundreds of stands displaying food from France and abroad. Wine producers are well represented and you'll find more than 100 stands for the French regions and their local produce.

On a smaller and friendlier scale is the **Salon Paris Fermier**, which brings together some 80 French producers of meat, cheese, honey and other foods in spring and 200 in autumn in the bucolic Parc Floral de Vincennes. The **Salon du Chocolat**, held in several world capitals, attracts around 130 chocolatiers from across the globe, some of whom team up with fashion designers to create extravagant chocolate dresses for the salon's fashion show.

Two yearly events celebrate the variety of cheese in Paris: the **Salon du Fromage et des Produits Laitiers** and the **Journée Nationale du Fromage**, both in March. The perfect place to stock up on gourmet items and luxury food gifts is the **Salon des Saveurs**, where you'll find goose foie gras from southwest France as well as saffron from Orléans. Proof of France's current enthusiasm for cooking classes is the **Cuisinez!** event, featuring cooking demonstrations and workshops by personalities such as TV chef Cyril Lignac, the French Jamie Oliver, and schools including l'Atelier des Chefs.

Fresh food delivery services

Food delivery has never been a big part of the French culture but that is changing. Supermarkets like Carrefour and Auchan deliver for a modest fee, or sometimes at no charge, a real boon if your apartment is accessible only by stairs.

The most interesting development has been the creation of delivery services for serious foodies who regret not having the time to shop in markets. **Le Haut du Panier** delivers vegetables supplied by the chefs' favourite market gardener, Joël Thiébault, right to your door each morning. You can't choose the contents of your box, and the more unusual vegetables like kohlrabi and striped beetroot are provided with suggested recipes. The company also delivers seasonal fruit from the Parc Naturel du Vexin outside Paris, cheese from Philippe Alléosse, bread from baker Jean-Luc Poujauran and coffee from Verlet. Other delivery services allow you to pick up your weekly basket at a drop-off point near your home or office. One such is the organic supplier **Les Paniers du Val de Loire**.

Première Etoile caters to time-deprived Parisians with sophisticated tastes by providing all the ingredients needed to prepare a meal for a given number of people along with recipes and pre-made desserts. The ingredients

10

Marie-Anne Cantin
cantin.fr

come from the same sources as those used by top Paris chefs. **Les Dîners de Bérénice** goes one step further, providing not only ingredients and recipes, but also tableware and utensils if you need them.

Ordering French food and wine online

If you live outside France but within Europe, there are still plenty of ways to get your French food fix. **Poilâne**'s rustic *pain au levain* keeps well enough to be shipped across the world – the bakery's director, Apollonia Poilâne, has it flown to her in Boston. Several Paris cheese shops, including **Marie-Anne Cantin** and **Alléosse**, take orders on their websites, as do some of the city's best chocolatiers. French olive oils are hard to find even in the best gourmet shops outside France, so it's worth placing an order with the Nice-based company **Oliviera**. Its founder, Nadim Beyrouti, seeks out the best olive oils in Provence every season and sells them for no more than a year to ensure they remain in peak condition. Since 1996, Isabelle de Montille, of the famous Burgundy family, has provided gourmet food at **www.goutsdefrance.com**.

For French wines there are several very professional sites. **Château Online** is aimed at the average wine enthusiast, while **Wine and Co** is geared more to the wine collector. The bigger wine sites offer significant discounts.

10

PLAT
du
JOUR

Food blogs

There is no shortage of information on dining in Paris – the only trick is sifting through it all and keeping current. One of the best ways to do this is to check into sites such as **eGullet** and **Chowhound**, in which food enthusiasts exchange notes on Paris dining. A particularly useful resource is the Paris digest on eGullet, in which John Talbott sums up everything written in the French press about Paris restaurants each week, with links to the original articles.

A number of entertaining blogs cover the Paris food scene, the best known of which are the whimsical **Chocolate and Zucchini** written by talented **Clotilde Dusoulier**, and pastry chef David Lebovitz's hilarious **Living the Sweet Life in Paris**, which is as much about the perks and perils of living in Paris as food itself. Chez Pim, written by San Franciscan Pim Techamuanvivit, is also lively and amusing with mouth-watering food photography. American baking expert **Dorie Greenspan**, the author of books on Paris pastries, has a particularly informative blog. Finally, for those who read French, opinionated **Gérard Poirot** does not shrink from critical reviews on chefs hyped by a generally complacent mainstream press and provides his readers with proper judgment on new openings.

10

Food and wine events

Cuisinez!
Late October
Musée du Louvre,
r de Rivoli, 1st
Ⓜ Palais Royal
salon-cuisinez.com
✛ 6/M9

Foire d'Automne
Mid October
Paris Expo, 15th
Ⓜ Porte de Versailles
foiredautomne.fr
✛ Off map

Foire de Paris
Late April
Paris Expo, Porte de
Versailles, 15th
Ⓜ Porte de Versailles
foiredeparis.fr
✛ Off map

**Journée Nationale
du Fromage**
March
Various locations in Paris
journeenationale
dufromage.com

Paris Fermier de Printemps
End March
Parc Floral de Paris, Bois
de Vincennes, Rte de la
Pyramide, 12th
Ⓜ Chateau de Vincennes
salonsfermiers.com
✛ Off map

Salon de l'Agriculture
Early March
Paris Expo, 15th
Ⓜ Porte de Versailles
salon-agriculture.com
✛ Off map

Salon du Chocolat
Mid-October
Paris Expo, 15th
Ⓜ Porte de Versailles
chocoland.com
✛ Off map

**Salon du Fromage et des
produits Laitiers**
Early March
Paris Expo, 15 th
Ⓜ Porte de Versailles
salon-fromage.com
✛ Off map

**Salon Mer et Vignes et
Gastronomie**
Mid-March
Paris Expo, 17th
Ⓜ Porte de Champerret
mer-et-vigne.fr
✛ 1/D1

Salon Paris Fermier
Mid-October
Parc Floral, Bois de
Vincennes, Rte de la Pyramide
Ⓜ Chateau de Vincennes
salonsfermiers.com
✛ Off map

Salon des Saveurs
Mid-May and early December
Paris Expo, Porte de
Champerret, 17th
Ⓜ Porte de Champerret
parisexpo.fr
✛ 1/D1

**Salon des Vignerons
Indépendants**
Late November
Paris Expo, 15th
Ⓜ Porte de Versailles
vigneron-independant.com
✛ Off map

**La Semaine Fraich'
Attitude**
Early June
Various locations in Paris
semainefraichattitude.com

La Semaine du Goût
Mid-October
Various locations in Paris
legout.com

Vivez Nature
May
Cité des Sciences et de
l'Industrie, La Villette, 19th
Ⓜ Porte de la Villette
vivez-nature.com
✛ Off map

Fresh food delivery services

Le Campanier
campanier.com

Les Diners de Bérénice
lesdinersdeberenice.fr

Paniers du Val de Loire
lespaniersduvaldeloire.fr

Carrefour supermarket
www.ooshop.com

Le Haut du Panier
lehautdupanier.com

Première Étoile
premiere-etoile.com

Ordering French food online

Alléosse
alleosse.com

La Maison du Chocolat
lamaisonduchocolat.com

Périgord black truffles
sainte-alvere.com

Goûts de France
goutsdefrance.com

Marie-Anne Cantin
cantin.fr

Poilâne
poilane.frm

Jean-Paul Hévin
www.jphevin.com

Oliviera
oliveira.com

Valette Foie Gras
valette.fr

Ordering French wine online

1855
1855.com

Château Online
chateauonline.com

Millesima
millesima.com

Bar Premium
barpremium.fr

iDealWine
idealwine.com

Wine & Co
wineandco.com

Food blogs

Chez Pim
chezpim.typepad.com

David Lebovitz
davidlebovitz.com

François Simon
francoissimon.typepad.fr

Chocolate & Zucchini
chocolateandzucchini.com

Dorie Greenspan
doriegreenspan.com

Gérard Poirot
restaurants.blog.lemonde.fr

Chowhound
chowhound.co

eGullet
egullet.org

Rosa Jackson
rosajackson.blogspot.com

10

See page 9
to scan the
directory

INDEX

Page numbers in italics refer to chapter directories

11

11

11

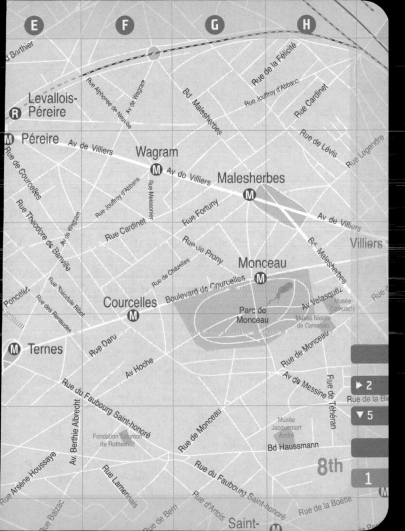

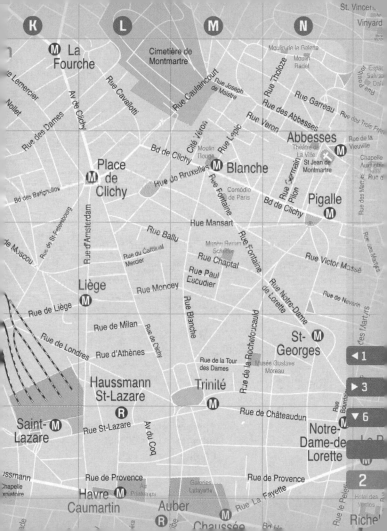

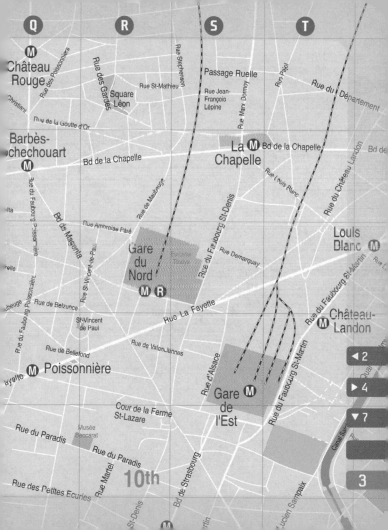

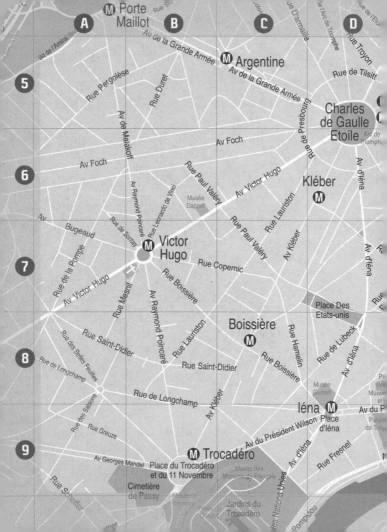

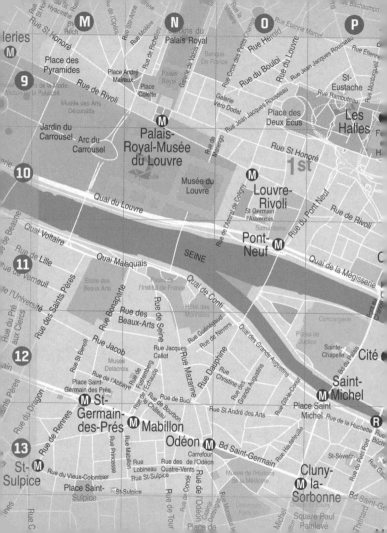

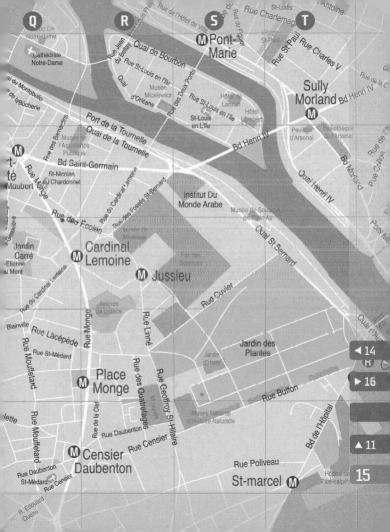

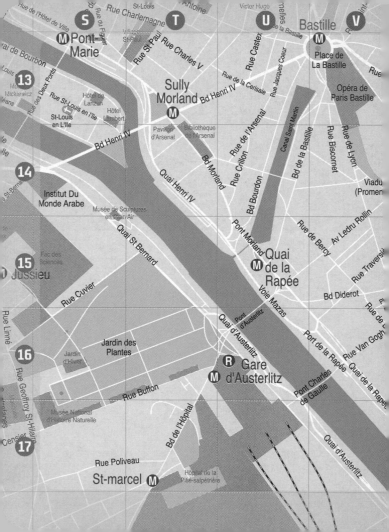

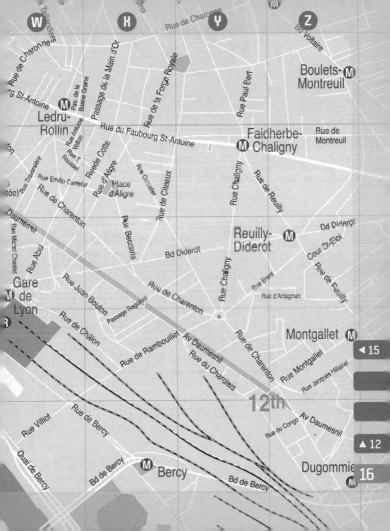

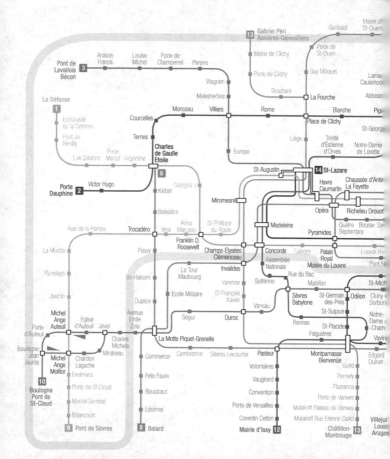

PARIS MET

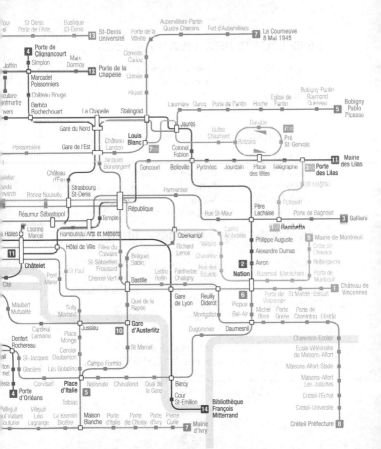

OTHER TITLES IN THE AUTHENTIK COLLECTION

Europe
Chic Paris
Artistik Paris

Gourmet London
Chic London
Artistik London

FORTHCOMING AUTHENTIK GUIDES – SPRING 2008

North America	Europe	Asia	Africa
Gourmet New York	Barcelona	Beijing	Marrakech
Chic New York	Berlin	Bali	Cape Town
Artistik New York	Milan		
	Prague		

FORTHCOMING WINE ROADBOOKS – AUTUMN 2008

France	Italy	North America
Bordeaux	Tuscany	Napa Valley
Burgundy		Sonoma County
Champagne	Spain	
Loire Valley	Rioja	

Visit www.authentikbooks.com
to find out more about AUTHENTIK titles

Rosa Jackson

Since her first visit to Paris at age four, Canadian-born Rosa Jackson has never tired of exploring the city's food markets and shops. She moved to France in 1995 to give culinary tours of the city and now designs food itineraries sur mesure. Since 2004 she has divided her time between Paris and Nice, where she teaches cooking in her 17th-century apartment, a few steps from the Cours Saleya market. Besides writing articles for international food magazines, Rosa has published two cookbooks in French, *Petites recettes pour grandir* and *La cuisine des paresseuses*.

Alain Bouldouyre

Gentleman artist Alain Bouldouyre captures in his fine line drawings what our *Gourmet Paris* author conjures up in words – the quintessence of the city. Art director for *Senso* magazine, and author/illustrator of numerous travel books, Alain fast-tracks around the world in hand-stitched loafers, a paintbox and sketch pad his most precious accessories. With bold yet sensitive brushstrokes he evokes Paris's treasures.

COMMERCIAL LICENSING

Authentik illustrations, text and listings are available for commercial licensing at www.authentikartwork.com.

ORIGINAL ARTWORK

All signed and numbered original illustrations by Alain Bouldouyre published in this book are available for sale. Original artwork by Alain Bouldouyre is delivered framed with a certificate of authenticity.

CUSTOM-MADE EDITIONS

Authentik books make perfect, exclusive gifts for personal or corporate purposes.

Special editions, including personalized covers, excerpts from existing titles and corporate imprints, can be custom produced.

All enquiries should be addressed to Wilfried LeCarpentier at wl@authentikbooks.com.

AUTHENTIK ®